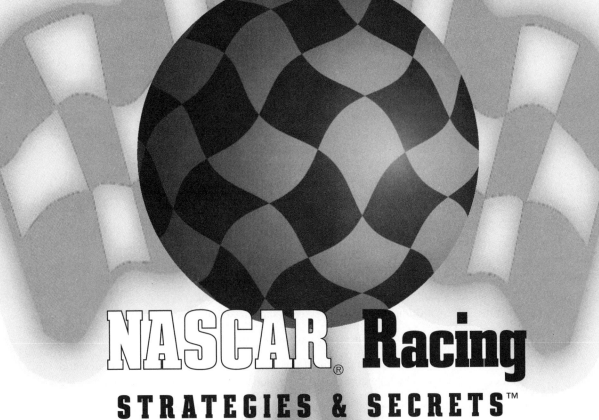

NASCAR® Racing

STRATEGIES & SECRETS™

LEE BUCHANAN

PAPYRUS™

SYBEX

SAN FRANCISCO   PARIS   DÜSSELDORF   SOEST

Acquisitions Manager	KRISTINE PLACHY
Product Manager	DAMON DEAN
Production Coordinator	LABRECQUE PUBLISHING SERVICES
Copy Editor	MARK WOODWORTH
Book Design and Production	WILLIAM SALIT
Proofreader	TORY MCLEARN
Cover Designer	ARCHER DESIGN

Dedication

This book is for racers everywhere, from you computer aces to the real heroes of NASCAR.

Acknowledgments

Hats off to Papyrus for creating a truly marvelous racing simulation. Writing about NASCAR Racing has been a joy. Thanks also to Damon Dean and the folks at Sybex, and to Tory McLearn and Lisa Labrecque at Labrecque Publishing. And special thanks to Peter Golenboch, whose book *American Zoom*, published by Macmillan Inc. is the most entertaining and colorful account of stock car racing that you'll find. The book is the source for most of my historical references.

CONTENTS AT A GLANCE

TABLE OF CONTENTS

7 GETTING THE MOST OUT OF NASCAR RACING....................172

INTRODUCTION
WHY WE RACE

IT'S **1975 AT HICKORY SPEEDWAY IN WESTERN NORTH** Carolina. In his orange '64 Chevelle, Harry Gant—the Taylorsville Flash—is in the midst of a nine-race winning streak at the ⅓-mile oval. On this Saturday night, they run a double feature, reversing the finishing order from the first race. Harry wins the first race easily, so he starts dead last in the second race. It doesn't matter. Harry picks off two or three cars a lap, passing inside and outside as he roars through the pack. Gant wins another, and I'm hooked—a racing fan for life.

Hickory had a great crop of racers then: Tommy Houston, Morgan Shepherd, and Ned Setzer battled Gant for supremacy. Hot-shot drivers would swagger into town like gunfighters on steamy Saturday nights in those days, looking to knock off the local heroes. Sam Ard up from Asheboro, Jack Ingram over from Asheville, Jimmy Hensley from Virginia. And later on, some kid named Dale Earnhardt.

Glory Days

A few years later, I joined the ranks of Gant and Earnhardt at Hickory. Well, sort of. I bought a beat-up '66 Chevelle and went racing in the rookie division. I finished 14th out of 18 cars that first night, and I didn't wreck. I was pretty pleased with myself as I went to pick up my prize money—$25 cash.

Another driver, a guy I'd blocked as he tried to pass me over the last couple of laps, eyed me in my shiny new driver's suit. "Who taught that boy how to drive?" sneered the big country boy, talking his way around a chaw of tobacco. It didn't matter. Man, I was a *racer*.

I drove about 15 races that summer, slammin' and bangin' with the good ol' boys every Saturday night. My best finish was sixth, but mostly I ran in the middle of the pack. We cheated a little with an oversized motor, but I still couldn't keep up with the leaders. I guess they cheated just a little more. Had second-place locked up in a heat race one night, but I spun out—all by

Figure 0.1
The author really did race stock cars. This, however, is just a dream. Actually, it's Buchanan before he turned a few laps at Charlotte Motor Speedway in the Richard Petty Driving Experience. (Photo by Michael Johnson)

myself—on the fourth turn of the last lap. In the last race, a couple of cars spun in front of me and I wiped out my Chevy. Like they say in those TV interviews, "It was just one of them racin' deals," but it was the end of my career.

Now, thanks to *NASCAR Racing* by Papyrus, I have a chance at the big time. And so do you. So put on your helmet, climb into the cockpit, tighten your belts, and fire up that engine. And remember: keep the shiny side up!

THE DRIVERS' MEETING

"Racers, Start Your Engines!"

NOTHING **QUITE EQUALS THE SPINE-TINGLING THRILL OF** racing. Thirty-nine drivers, all with 700 horsepower under the hood, and all desperate to be in front. They'll take chances, and they aren't afraid to bang fenders as they jostle for position at top speed, side-by-side and inches apart. They're all hungry and determined to win. And that's just the rush-hour traffic, as people race home to do a little *NASCAR Racing* on the computer.

Once you get there, you're in for some of the hottest computer action you'll find, as you match driving skills and mechanical know-how with NASCAR's best. This is big-time stock-car racing. If you can win consistently, without cheating, who knows? Forget the game—you just might be able to run with the big boys.

YOU NEED THIS BOOK

It's fun to play, but understand this *NASCAR Racing* ain't no arcade game. Shoot, I feel like spittin' some tobacco juice just thinkin' about arcade racing games. *NASCAR Racing* is the *real thing*. If it was any more realistic, Papyrus might have to pay prize money.

In computer simulations, realism usually equals difficulty. *NASCAR Racing* is the most demanding and accurate computer simulation I've ever played. True, you can have some thrills by just jumping in and hitting the gas, but to really squeeze the most enjoyment out of this sim, you have to work at it.

With lots of practice—and the help of this book—you'll progress just like a rookie on the NASCAR circuit, from an also-ran to running with the leaders. When you're able to race door-to-door for the lead with opponents at full strength, there's just nothing like it.

NASCAR Racing puts you in the driver's seat for the hottest racing action around. The real tracks, the real drivers, the real thing. This simulation is so good—and some actual NASCAR racers like to play it, too—that you can really gauge how you might perform behind the wheel of a 700-horsepower race car.

And, because it's so realistic, *NASCAR Racing* is tough to master. You've got to get your hands dirty in the garage, and then run hundreds of miles of practice to fine-tune both your car and your driving skills. Finally, you put it all together on race day—with 38 other cars on the track. Sure, it's fun to run a few laps and get into a spectacular wreck, but if you're a racer, then you want to win against the toughest competition—with opponents at 100%, long races, and no driver aids.

WHAT'S IN THIS BOOK

This book will help you get to the winner's circle. I'll show you how to develop the fastest car set-ups, and then show you how to tweak them to suit your own driving style. You'll learn the quickest line around each race track, where to pass, when to pit, and how to win. And I'll show you where to get cool car graphics, lightning-fast set-ups, plus lots of utilities to help you get the most out of *NASCAR Racing*.

If you just can't get up to speed, check out Chapter 2. You'll find an in-depth look at every aspect of tires, chassis set-up, weight transfer, and power performance. There's an easy-to-use chart that will help you cure any handling problem.

If you're running fast, but you can't keep your car from slamming the concrete—or your fellow drivers—then see Chapter 3. You'll learn not just how to be fast, but also how to survive and win.

Can't quite keep up with the leaders? In Chapter 4, I'll show you how to get smart and win races on pit strategy alone.

Your car's not the only thing that needs to be fast in *NASCAR Racing*. There are ways to fine-tune your computer, too, to get the most out of this game. Chapter 7 will show you how to super-charge your system.

And when you get tired of blowing the doors off the computer-controlled cars, Chapter 8 will get you ready to take on a faster and more dangerous opponent—other guys like you—in modem and network racing.

SAY HELLO TO PAPYRUS

Before you drive your way to fame and wealth, let me introduce you to some of the people at Papyrus Design Group who have made this bit of vicarious glory possible.

Let's be honest about this. The Papyrus team is a great group of guys and gals, but they hide a pretty dark secret. They're *IndyCar Racing* fans. That's right, the people who crafted an almost perfect simulation of stock-car racing are really fans of those "flying fuel tanks," as the NASCAR crowd likes to call the Indy cars. (Just kidding, of course.) Papyrus is hard at work on *IndyCar Racing II* as I write this, and I can't wait to get my hands on it.

The Papyrus designers weren't raised on grits and grease and stock-car racing. In fact, most members of the team—including designer Adam Levesque and lead programmer John Wheeler—weren't race fans at all when the company started. Still, they managed to create the most authentic racing simulation ever seen.

The driving force behind Papyrus is co-founder Dave Kaemmer. He grew up in Indiana, so his interest in racing came naturally. Kaemmer was into computers early on. He started programming while in college, and he knew what he wanted to do: write computer games.

Kaemmer took an idea for a racing simulation to publisher Electronic Arts, and in 1989 the *Indianapolis 500* sim hit the market. The game wasn't a huge seller, but it hit home with an appreciative audience and attracted a lot of attention within the industry.

"It was sort of a cult hit," Kaemmer says. "A lot of people inside the industry knew about and liked it. That helped us get *IndyCar Racing* under way."

Figure 1.1
The Papyrus
Design Group

Kaemmer and company set the tone immediately for their racing sims: forget the arcade stuff—we want *realism*.

"I wanted to create games that put the player in the seat of a race car," Kaemmer notes. "I wanted, as much as possible, to get away from the arcade-like racing game. I wanted to do something that was real racing, where you're out at the limit of adhesion, trying to figure out how to scratch your way by another car, by figuring out where he's fast and where he's not. We try to re-create the mental concentration that a real race driver must have, driving each lap the same, right at the limit of control."

IndyCar Racing, released in 1993, was the big hit Papyrus needed. The next step, Kaemmer says, was obvious. "We figured a NASCAR game would be a natural follow-up."

How realistic is *NASCAR Racing*? Bobby Labonte, a rising star on the NASCAR circuit, manages to find a bit of time in his schedule to play the game. According to him and others, the sim has been accepted and praised in NASCAR's inner circle as a realistic simulation of the sport.

Yet even Papyrus wasn't prepared for this game's success. Based on a sport still considered largely regional in its appeal, the game became one of the biggest hits in computer gaming. "The sales of *NASCAR Racing* have been phenomenal. Part of it has to do with the popularity of NASCAR itself, but the game has also sold well in Europe, where few people follow NASCAR," Kaemmer says.

Dave Kaemmer's enthusiasm for the sport, as well as his devotion to realism, are reflected in the team he has built at Papyrus. Sure, they probably spend part of their work days playing games, but we can forgive them. They've worked and played hard to produce the best racing sim in the world.

John Wheeler was lead programmer on the NASCAR project, involved in both writing the program code and designing the game itself.

"I started at the beginning of *IndyCar Racing*, in December of 1992," Wheeler recalls. "Like 95 percent of us, I was not a race fan. The first week I was working here, I watched a couple of videotapes. One that really struck me was an IndyCar race at Phoenix, this one-mile oval with guys diving in and out of traffic at incredibly high speeds. I was hooked."

For Wheeler, the most satisfying reaction to the game has come from the racing community itself. "The realism is the most important thing, and lots of people in racing are psyched about this product," he comments.

You said it, John. We're psyched, and we're ready to race. But before we begin, tip your Richard Petty cowboy hat toward Massachussetts in a gesture of thanks to the talented folks at Papyrus. Now get ready to start your engines . . .

THE GARAGE

Down 'n' Dirty

OK, **HOT SHOT—BEFORE YOU CLIMB INTO THE COCKPIT AND BLOW** the doors off NASCAR's best, you've got to earn your way into the driver's seat. So roll up your sleeves and get ready to get some dirt under those fingernails. It's time to learn your way around the garage.

You may not feel at *home* in the garage. In fact, you may not know a sway bar from a bar of soap. Even if you have no interest in becoming a master mechanic, you should at least learn what makes your car go. I'll give you some fast set-ups, but none will be as fast as a set-up tweaked especially for your own driving style.

No one knows better than the driver how a car is behaving on the track. Even if you don't care about down force and torque, or about drag and camber, you'll still benefit from a basic understanding of car set-up. And where can you turn for advice when your car suddenly gets dangerously loose? You can only turn to your knowledge of your equipment and your own instincts.

CHOOSE YOUR WEAPONS

Direct involvement by automakers in the United States is not as intense today as it was in the 1960s, although GM and Ford are still very much a part of the sport. The reason is simple, the automakers reason: win on Sunday (with the world watching), sell on Monday.

Brand loyalty is greater among NASCAR fans than in any other form of auto racing, and it's usually a family tradition, an allegiance as strong as blood. My dad was a Chevy man, so I naturally stepped in line. I've never owned a Chevrolet, and I drive (gasp!) a Honda now—but when it comes down to a battle between Chevy and Ford, in my mind it's no contest.

You're probably not bound by that sort of blind, redneck loyalty to a make of car, so you should test drive the three

Figure 2.1
The Lumina isn't the best race car ever fielded by Chevrolet, but you can still win with it.

available models before you choose. They're separated only by slight differences in handling characteristics. And if you want to blame your pathetic performances on your car, you can always change horses in midseason.

Quick, name the model that ruled NASCAR racing in the early 1950s. Chevy? Ford? How about Chrysler? Nope. Try the mighty Hudson Hornet. Powered by a 6-cylinder, twin-carb engine, the Hudsons took the season championship from 1951 through 1954, winning 79 races in the process. The Hornet was fast enough, but it was the car's unique chassis design that made it virtually unbeatable. A system of wraparound frame rails allowed the body to sit closer to the ground, giving the Hudson a lower center of gravity and superior handling characteristics in the turns.

PIT STOP

CHEVROLET LUMINA

The Lumina hasn't been one of Chevrolet's better race cars, and by the 1995 season it has been replaced by the sleeker Monte Carlo after being consistently outrun by the Ford

Figure 2.2
The Ford T-Bird might be your best choice, especially when you're learning the ropes.

Thunderbird. In the game, the Lumina has slightly more rear downforce, making it a tick faster than the Thunderbird down the straightaways of longer race tracks.

If you'd rather climb aboard the Monte Carlo, you can use the Paint Kit to touch up the detail of the Lumina to make it closely resemble the newer Chevy. If you're not much of a graphics artist, and you have access to an on-line service such as CompuServe, you'll find several car-sets, uploaded by other racers, that include the new cars. See Chapter 9 for details on the many tools and graphics that are available on-line.

FORD THUNDERBIRD

The clean lines of the T-Bird have helped make this car one of the most successful race cars in recent memory. The Thunderbird has more than held its own against Chevy since Bill Elliott tore the circuit to shreds in the late '80s.

In the game, slightly better front-end downforce makes the Ford a stout short-track car, while it may trail the Lumina down the faster straightaways.

Figure 2.3
The Pontiac is a solid compromise between speed and handling.

PONTIAC GRAND PRIX

If you can't choose between the Chevy and the Ford, you should take the Pontiac for a test drive. The Grand Prix is a stable race car, somewhere between the Lumina and the Thunderbird. NASCAR rule changes made the Grand Prix more competitive in the 1995 season, but of course that won't help you here. Give it a spin; Pontiac could use some more teams on the circuit.

ANY CAR WILL DO

Car selection is largely a matter of personal preference, so don't agonize too much over the decision. There's no magic make of car that will transform you from a back-marker to a front-runner. Until you get a feel for how the car is behaving on the track, you won't be able to distinguish among the three models.

If you're just starting out and can't decide which car you want to drive to wealth and glory, choose the Ford Thunderbird. The slightly greater downforce makes the T-Bird a little more stable on the shorter tracks, yet won't slow the car appreciably on the superspeedways. If your momma drives a

Chevrolet, though, you'd better think again before she gets on your tail about it.

WHERE THE RUBBER MEETS THE ROAD

Good slogan, but the wrong company. When Papyrus developed the game, there was a tire war raging in NASCAR. Goodyear has long dominated the sport, but in 1994, race-tire specialist Hoosier developed tires for NASCAR's premier division and set off a controversial competition that saw the companies pushing the limits of tire performance. Tires got faster, but drivers worried that safety was being sacrificed for speed. Hoosier pulled out of the sport after the 1994 season, and now Goodyear once again is the unchallenged tire source.

Since the game is based on the 1994 season, however, you still have a choice. In the game, Hoosiers have slightly better grip, so they run a shade faster than the Goodyears. Better grip also means greater wear, so you'll have to change 'em more often than the steadier Goodyears.

Most of your competitors run Goodyears. Pay attention during green-flag pit stops and you can pick out the ones running Hoosiers. They'll be forced to pit several laps before the Goodyear-shod cars.

TIP Since you're also the racing commissioner, you can force everyone to run Goodyears—or Hoosiers, for that matter. If you're a stickler for realism, make 'em run Goodyears. That will help put all the cars on the same pit-stop sequence, though some will pit earlier or later anyway.

TURNING THE WRENCHES

Most of the NASCAR greats were also ace mechanics and chassis experts. They *had* to be. In the early days, your pit crew might consist of your brother-in-law and a couple of the guys who hung out down at the gas station. You built the car, set up the chassis, lifted some spare parts, turned the wrenches, and then you raced it. And when you wrecked, you were up all night hammering out the dents.

Today, there's a different breed of driver—the hired guns who just show up at the track to race. They get all of the glory and none of the grunge. So which do you want to be?

The beauty of *NASCAR Racing* is that you aren't forced into one role. You can put on the hat of the old-style driver, turning the wrenches in the garage, and then turning the wheel on the track. Or you can be one of the new-generation pretty boys, eager to get to the victory lane so that you can do a TV interview surrounded by babes

You can run fast—and win plenty of races—just by loading the hot set-ups. But one thing's certain: you'll be a faster and better driver on the track *if* you've done your time and got some grease under your nails in the garage.

THE QUEST FOR SPEED

The process of setting up a race car has two fundamental stages: making adjustments in the garage, and testing on the race track. Too bad it's not as simple as it sounds! It's a long, laborious, and maybe even boring process. Run the car 20 laps, see how it's handling, and then adjust the rear weight bias by a percentage point or two. Run 20 more laps, check the tire temperatures, and put in another pound of air. Then it's 20 more laps, check temps, and make another tiny adjustment. That's why when these guys aren't racing, they're practicing. You'll find precious little free time in the big leagues of racing.

It's just a game, I know, but if you're serious about car set-up, you have to approach it the same way. There's nothing wrong with jumping into the game, loading somebody else's set-up, and taking the green flag. Heck, that's what most of the real drivers do these days. This section, however, is for players who want to get into the guts of the simulation—for the motorheads who want to try to squeeze another two-tenths of a second out of their lap times.

TIP
Save your set-ups as you go, deleting old files to avoid confusion. Start with the stock Ace set-up (or another one you like better), run enough laps to get the tires nice and hot, and then note your fastest speed. Let's say you're at Bristol and you run 121.234 mph. Save that set-up as 1212, then begin your work with a single adjustment, maybe a stiffer right-front shock. Go back out, run the same number of laps, and check your fastest speed again. If it's faster, say 122.106—and feels fairly comfortable to drive—save the new set-up as 1221. Delete the old file or keep it as a backup. Repeat the process with your next adjustment, saving each one that's faster than the one before.

The single most important thing to keep in mind: never make more than one adjustment at a time. If you stiffen the right-front shock and lower the air pressure in that same tire, and then discover the tire's overheating after several laps, you won't know which adjustment is causing the problem, or whether it's the combination of changes. This method of checking variables—limiting yourself to making one adjustment at a time—may be time-consuming, but it's less confusing and will pay off in results..

PRACTICE PERFECT

In between adjustments, of course, you'll take the car out on the track to see how it behaves. It's critical that you approach each of these practice sessions the same way. Run the identical number of laps, and "go for it" to the same degree for each session. The tire temperature readings will be meaningless unless you run a sufficient number of laps to get the tires up to racing temperature. Run at least 5 laps on the short tracks, and

Figure 2.4
Tires are your
friend. Take care
of them if you
want to win.

10 on the longer tracks (1.5 miles or more). It sounds screwy, I know, running more laps on longer tracks—but the tires heat up faster in the turns, and you're in the turns most of the time on the short tracks.

Get in the habit of checking the tire temps at the same point on the track. Immediately on exiting a turn is a good place, since the tires should be hottest there. As always, use the Pause button when you take your eyes off the track for more than a split second. Try to run consistent laps as you work on your set-up, braking and getting back on the gas at the same places on the track.

TIRES: YOUR LINK TO THE TRACK

"How are the tires holdin' up?" That's probably the most frequently heard question in the garage area of a NASCAR race. Aside from your driving ability, tires are the single most important factor determining your car's speed and handling characteristics. While you can't change the tires—except for swapping brands—every adjustment you make to the chassis has an impact *on* the tires.

HOT AND COLD

Tire temperatures are the one constant factor in all your garage work. With the exception of aerodynamics and wheel lock, every aspect of car set-up influences—and is influenced by—tire temps. You'll constantly be chasing these numbers, so get used to it.

Temperature is measured at three points on the racing surface of the tire: inside, middle, and outside. That means the tire is gripping evenly across its surface, giving it a more stable "footprint" on the racing surface. Your goal is to get tire temps within an acceptable range and even across the tire. Ideally, you want even tire temps in a range of 200–225 degrees. Below that range, the tire isn't gripping as well as it could. Run hotter than 225 and you shorten the life of that tire. You'll never reach the peak temperatures on all four tires, even though that's your goal.

PERFORMING UNDER PRESSURE

In general terms, lower air pressure makes a tire stick better and run hotter, while higher pressure results in cooler temps and less grip. Below an acceptable pressure—it varies based on other adjustments—the outside temperatures will run hotter than the middle. Above that range, the middle of the tire will get hotter than the outside temps.

TIP Start with the pressures in the Ace set-up, but these are usually in the low end of the acceptable range. You can usually increase the pressure by three or four pounds from the Ace setting and maintain even temperatures. This should cool the tire slightly and extend its life, without losing any grip.

On most tracks, the right-side tires take the burden of the car's weight as it travels through left-handed turns. You'll often be battling hot tire temps on that side of the car, so bumping up the pressure slightly may be an easy fix. The left-side tires, by contrast, often don't get hot enough, especially the left front. Try lowering the pressure there to build some more heat. On many tracks, though, you'll never be able to get the left-front tire temp into the desired range.

TIP Tire temperatures are affected by a number of factors, including your driving line. As you get faster through the corners, the tires will run hotter and are more likely to build heat on the outside. A set-up that worked fine at Martinsville turning laps at 88 mph may be abusing the tires if you've turned it up to 93 mph. That's why you shouldn't worry about set-up until you've learned your way around a particular track.

STAGGER

Running slightly larger tires on the right side enhances the ability of the car to turn in the corners. The right-side tires actually have to travel a greater distance on the outside of a turn than the left-side tires, which are taking the shorter route on the inside. With no "stagger," the right-side tires have to work harder—actually turning faster—than those on the inside. To compensate for this, you can put tires on the right side with a slightly greater diameter. This enables them to travel the greater distance in fewer revolutions.

If your car is pushing in the turns (understeer) on an oval track, try increasing the stagger setting slightly. This should help you turn left more easily. Don't go too far with the stagger, though. Too much of a size difference between the left- and right-side tires will cause the car to pull too hard to the left, scrubbing off speed and increasing wear on the tires.

Stagger is effective only on the ovals, where you're turning left all day. You'll want a neutral setting here on the road

Figure 2.5
Racing on the ovals means all left-hand turns. Larger tires on the right side will help the car turn more easily.

courses, maybe even a slightly negative setting to help with tough right-hand corners. Stagger works best on the short tracks, where you spend most of your time in the corners. You'll want less stagger on superspeedways.

As with most other adjustments, changing stagger has a ripple effect on other settings. Camber, in particular, will require another look after you change the stagger. Run a few hot laps and check tire temps, and then make another camber adjustment.

CAMBER

The term "camber" denotes an angle adjustment to the front wheels that determines how those tires make contact with the track while cornering. Take a look at the camber graphic of the right-front shown here or on the screen when you're in the garage. If that tire is making even contact with the ground when the car's at a standstill, what will happen when the car slams into the banking at high speed, and all that weight shifts to the right side? That's right, Billy. The outside edge of the tire will

Figure 2.6
The camber
setting affects
how the tires
make contact
with the track.

take most of the weight, while the inner half may be barely
gripping the track at all. Not good.

To compensate, you can adjust the camber, or the angle of
the tire to the track. A neutral setting means the tire is perpendicular to the ground. That's fine when the car's parked, but it
won't work for high-speed cornering. By increasing that
angle—actually tilting the wheel slightly inward—you prepare
the wheel for the conditions it will experience under high-speed
cornering.

SETTING CAMBER

Camber is measured in degrees: zero degrees is perpendicular
to the ground; a positive reading tilts the wheel outward; a negative reading tilts the wheel inward. Don't worry about a positive reading—you'll never use one. Rather, your job is to find
the degree of negative camber required to produce even tire
temps at a given track.

Run several laps in practice to get the tires up to racing temperature, and then Pause the game after you exit a turn and
check the temps. If the outside reading is higher than the middle

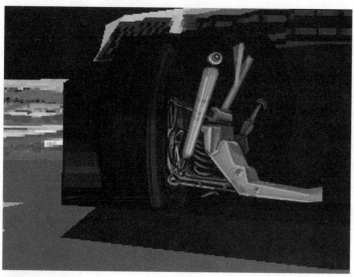

Figure 2.7
The stiffness of the shocks helps determine how weight is transferred.

and inner temps, reduce the amount of negative camber. If the inner part of the tire is hotter, increase the setting. As always, make slight adjustments until you get a feel for how the changes affect the readings.

SUSPENSION
SHOCK TREATMENT

In racing, shock absorbers do a bit more than helping to smooth out the bumps in the road. You're looking for high-speed handling, not a smooth ride. By stiffening and softening a wheel's shocks, you can adjust how much weight is transferred to that wheel in relation to the others. This can have a drastic impact on a car's handling characteristics and tire temperatures, so treat these babies with respect. Keep shock adjustments to a minimum, unless your set-up is way off and you're looking for a major chassis change.

WORK ON THE TEMPS
Shocks are a good place to start when you're trying to get tire temperatures into the desired range. It depends on the track,

of course, but the right-front tire is almost always the trouble spot on an oval track. If the right-front is running dangerously hot, soften the spring to put less weight on that corner of the car in the turns. The left-front, on the other hand, almost always runs well below the 220–225 degree range. If you can't get enough heat into that tire, set the shock to 100% stiffness. Work with the shocks all the way around the car—remember, one change at a time—trying to get the tire temps as close together as you can, and within the desired range.

GETTING A HANDLE

Shocks also help determine how your car behaves in the corners. If the car is pushing, soften the shocks on the front wheels to get better grip up front, or stiffen the rear shocks, or try a combination of front and rear adjustments. To help cure a loose situation, try the reverse: stiffer front shocks and/or softer shocks in the rear.

TIP When you're just earning your NASCAR driver's license, you may want to go with softer shock settings all the way around. The transference of weight from wheel to wheel will be a bit slower, giving you more time to react. Later on, when you get more skilled behind the wheel, you'll want to stiffen the suspension. The weight transfer will be more abrupt through the corners, giving you finer control, though it's much easier to lose control if you're not ready.

DIALING IT IN

After you've come up with a stable, fast set-up, you can make minor adjustments to the shocks to change how your car behaves at various points on a race track. It's important to remember, though, that we're talking about fine-tuning the chassis here. Don't try this until you already have a solid set-up.

First, let's look at what happens as your car goes through a turn. As you enter a corner, the car decelerates and begins to lean to the outside. Weight shifts to the right side (on an oval), and thus to the shocks on the right-front and right-rear wheels. As you accelerate off the corner, that weight rolls back over the center of the chassis, and the left-side shocks are absorbing a greater share of the weight.

It's common for the car to push straight ahead (it doesn't want to turn) when entering a turn. To help cure this problem, soften the right-front shock and/or stiffen the left-rear shock. This should increase the grip of the right-front tire and help you steer low when entering the corners.

The car is often loose coming off a turn, with the rear end losing traction. To ease this condition, stiffen the left-front shock and/or soften the left-rear shock. This will tighten the chassis coming off the turn without creating a "push" when entering the turn.

WEDGE

Let's get this straight right away: those pretty Indy boys may call it cross weight, but in NASCAR it's called "wedge." So enough of that cross-weight talk here. You're in NASCAR country!

Consider wedge adjustments a quick fix to what's ailing your car's handling. Wedge is a way of varying the amount of weight carried by the right-front and left-rear wheels. By decreasing, or taking out, wedge, you can help alleviate a push or understeer condition. Increasing the wedge setting tightens up the car, helping to cure a loose condition.

Think of a table with the left-rear and right-front legs a tad shorter than the others. You can tip the table slightly toward either of those shorter legs. And after the Thanksgiving turkey slides onto the floor, you fold up a piece of paper and stick it under one of the legs to stabilize the table. That's sort of how wedge works, tilting the chassis slightly toward the left-rear or the right-front.

> **TIP**
> When first setting up a car on a track during pre-season testing, use shocks, left bias, and rear bias to come up with a good chassis set-up. Try to leave wedge at 50%, or neutral, in this initial set-up. Then when you come to the track on race day, you can use wedge adjustments to "dial in" the car based on the current weather and track conditions. Wedge is also your most valuable adjustment during pit stops, so try to save it for adapting to conditions during the race.

WEIGHT MANAGEMENT

Weight transfer is the key to how your tires react under high-speed conditions, and therefore how well your car handles through the turns.

To get a feel for how these various adjustments work, you have to understand the dynamics at work as your car races around a track at high speed. The same forces are in play when you're driving your mini-van to the grocery store, but they are magnified a bit when you're roaring into turns at 190 mph, at the very edge of control.

We tend to think of weight or gravity as an unchanging natural force, but when an object is in motion, it's more accurate to think of weight as fluid energy. The 3,500-pound object that is your race car is in a constant state of flux as it barrels around the track. When you hit the gas, weight is shifted to the rear of the car. Mash the brake pedal, and that weight is thrown forward. And as the car rounds a curve, weight is transferred to the side of the car on the outside of the turn.

The vast majority of your set-up time is devoted to controlling and compensating for this weight transference. Left bias, rear bias, and cross-weight adjustments are meant to minimize these shifts in weight, thus making the car more comfortable to drive. That's enough technical stuff, huh? (Jeez, I'm sure glad racing doesn't involve chemistry . . .)

TIP Work on your race set-up with about a half-tank of fuel in the tank. If you come up with a blazing fast set-up on a full load of fuel, the car's handling is likely to go away as the race wears on and you burn fuel.

LEFT BIAS

Since most of the NASCAR boys—and an occasional gal—do most of their turning to the left, chassis experts put as much of the weight as they can on the left side of the car, to the inside of the turn. Each car must weigh in at inspection at a minimum of 3,500 pounds, but the teams have some discretion about how they achieve that weight. The car can be as light as the teams can build it, then the extra weight can be moved around the chassis to achieve the desired effect on handling.

Of course, nobody's ever bolted a lead bar under the dashboard to get through pre-race inspection, and then removed it before the race started. That would be cheating.

The left-bias setting determines how much of that weight goes to the left side of the car. This is no high-tech solution. The weight consists of bars of lead or titanium, bolted to the frame.

The solution here is simple: start out by setting left bias all the way to the legal limit on the ovals. On the shortest tracks, you'll probably want to keep it to the maximum setting. For the superspeedways, where you spend much less time in the corners, try shifting a bit of the weight to the right, but keep these adjustments very slight.

The road courses are a different story. On both Watkins Glen and Sears Point, there are more right turns than left turns, so you'll want more weight on the right side. Don't go over-board shifting weight to the right, though, because you have to turn left some, too.

REAR BIAS

No, this doesn't mean you don't like people's butts. (Well, maybe you don't, but that's your business.) Our business here is *racing*, and rear bias refers to the amount of weight that you pre-load into the front and rear areas of the chassis. Rear bias can have a tremendous impact on how the car behaves during acceleration and braking. In general, moving weight forward will tighten the car, while shifting weight to the rear will make the car looser.

At 3,500 pounds, a 50% rear-bias setting is neutral, with 1,750 pounds each in the front and rear of the car. On high-speed tracks, the near-constant acceleration moves some of that weight to the rear, which tends to make the car loose. By starting out with more of the weight at the rear of the car, you can reduce the effect of that weight transference under racing conditions. At shorter tracks, you'll want less of the weight in the rear, since you're not accelerating as much. Remember, though, these are very slight adjustments, and you'll probably want slightly more weight in the front at any track.

As driver Dave Marcis says in the manual, "The front percentage of the race car, at, say, Talladega would perhaps be around 52.5 to 53 percent. If you were at a race track like Martinsville, the front percentage of the car would only be about 50.5 to 51 percent." Thanks, Dave.

WHEEL LOCK

This setting determines how sharply the front wheels turn when you crank on the steering wheel or the joystick. It's largely a matter of personal preference, but I find the stock set-tings—15 degrees—far too high. A slight jerk on the wheel can turn you straight into the wall. Ay, caramba!

Adjust the setting downward to whatever level feels com-fortable. I like a wheel lock of 9 or 10 degrees. Make sure you

Figure 2.8
Wheel lock determines steering sensitivity. It's largely a matter of comfort and personal preferance.

can get it adjusted sharply enough to make each turn, of course—but since you aren't going to be doing a three-point turn on the race track, keep this value as low as you can get by with. Come to think of it, you might have to make a three-point turn when your mangled car is resting up against the outside wall, pinned beside another car, but you won't be too concerned with wheel lock.

GEARING

The gear ratios determine how many RPMs your engine turns, and thus how fast your car can go. For the oval tracks—with the exception of Pocono—you're really only concerned about fourth gear, since you don't change gears except when taking the green flag. The road courses are another matter; we'll look at gearing for those later on.

GEARING FOR THE OVALS

The manual suggests setting a fourth-gear ratio that revs high enough to cause the red warning light on the tachometer to

Figure 2.9
The lower the gear ratio, the more RPMs your engine will turn

come on at the end of the longest straightaway, but's it's not quite that simple. True, this is a good rule for the short tracks, where you're more concerned with quick acceleration off the corners than pure speed at the end of the straightaways. Your lap times on a track like Martinsville, though, are more dependent on acceleration and cornering speed than on straightaway speeds. On those tracks, you want the tach light to come on just before you begin braking for the corner—at least on your fastest laps. If you're hitting 9,000 rpms while you're taking it easy, however, you'll risk blowing the engine when you really need to stand on the gas. The same idea applies at the one-mile tracks, though straightaway speed is more of a concern there, so you have to balance the need for top-end speed versus the need for acceleration.

At the tracks of 1.5 miles and longer, the balance between speed and acceleration leans toward speed, especially at Talladega. Your car's engine generates more acceleration at 8,000 rpms than it does at 9,000 rpms. Forget for a moment about over-revving and damaging the engine. Even if you couldn't hurt the engine, you wouldn't want to red-line the tach for more than a couple of seconds at the end of a straightaway, because the car is no longer accelerating.

The tachometer's red line is 9,000 rpms, but you should almost never reach that point on a superspeedway; you should be *approaching* 9,000 rpms by the time you let off the gas.

> **TIP**
>
> Don't limit your speed by a fourth-gear ratio that's too short. As you learn your way around a track, your line will get better and you'll pick up speed because your driving skills are improving. Let's say you're running Atlanta, and the tach light is flashing at the end of the front stretch heading into turn 1. You think you're running pretty hot laps, maybe in the 175 mph range. But as you run more laps, you find you can stay in the throttle a split-second longer going into turn 1. Now you're clicking off laps at 177 mph and reaching 9,000 rpms. That's putting a greater strain on the engine and limiting your top-end speed. It's a good idea to leave yourself a little cushion in the gearing to allow yourself to get faster.

NASCAR Racing faithfully models just about every aspect of a stock car's performance, including the consequences of over-revving the engine. You can shorten the fourth-gear ratio slightly from the stock Ace set-up for most tracks, but you shouldn't go much further. The dashboard gauges work, too, so you can watch what happens if you insist on pushing the powerplant past the breaking point. The oil pressure will drop and the water temperature will soar, and then . . . silence. Next thing you know you'll be standing in the pits, quaking in your boots while talking to a TV reporter: "Well, Glenn, we were just ridin' along there, waitin' for the last 100 miles to make our move, when the engine blew. We'll get 'em next week."

Figure 2.10
The rear spoiler setting is a trade-off between speed and handling stability.

AERODYNAMICS

Of course, stock cars aren't stock anymore, but their bodies *must* have the same shape and dimensions as the cars on the showroom floors. NASCAR officials use templates to make sure race cars comply. As a result, these stock cars aren't the aerodynamic missiles of, say, the IndyCar or Grand Prix circuits. Instead, the race teams in NASCAR have to depend on the automakers in Detroit to come up with sleek designs. Teams are limited to front and rear spoilers when they want to make changes to the flow of air over the car.

REAR SPOILER

This thin strip of metal on the rear-deck lid has a tremendous effect on your car's performance. As air rushes over the car, it catches on the rear spoiler, creating downforce. That downforce makes the car more stable and lets it handle better, but it bleeds off speed. The higher the spoiler angle, the greater the downforce. A lower angle reduces this effect, increasing speed at the cost of handling stability.

Figure 2.11
The front air dam
is usually at the
lowest setting.

At the faster superspeedways, you'll want a low rear-spoiler setting, while the short tracks require a high spoiler angle. The emphasis on top speed at Talladega requires the lowest allowable rear-spoiler angle. The slowest track, Martinsville, demands the maximum spoiler angle, 70 degrees.

The rest of the tracks fall somewhere between these extremes. You'll have to make the call, whether you want to sacrifice some straightaway speed for a more stable, better-handling race car. As you get faster and more confident at a track, try reducing the spoiler angle to see if you can gain some speed and still be able to handle the car comfortably in traffic. Be careful, though! Some of the faster tracks, like Charlotte and Atlanta, demand both speed and stable handling in the corners. Trim the rear spoiler too much at those tracks and you'll get a taste of concrete.

FRONT SPOILER

The front spoiler, or air dam, catches air at the bottom-front of the car, creating downforce that pushes the front-end of the car down to the track. You'll almost always want the front spoiler set all the way down to increase stability. Talladega is again the exception to the rule. There, the need for speed requires a higher front-spoiler setting to reduce drag. Start with the front air dam set to the maximum height. But if you're smokin' the rest of the field at Talladega (and you should), experiment with a lower setting to see if it makes the car easier to drive, especially through the tricky tri-oval.

The brief but spectacular run of the muscle cars added some color to the automotive scene in the late 1960s, both for hot rods on the streets and on the race tracks of NASCAR. The high-winged, aerodynamically designed Dodge Charger, Plymouth Superbird, Ford Torino, and Mercury Cyclone took factory involvement to new heights—and took "stock" car racing to unheard-of speeds. In 1968, a young Cale Yarborough sped around Daytona in a Wood Brothers Mercury at 189.222 mph, nearly 10 mph faster than the previous one-lap record. • By then, of course, there was very little that was "stock" about these stock cars. The automakers adhered to the letter, if not the spirit, of NASCAR rules by producing a few hundred of these high-speed models for the general public. Afraid that the sport was moving away from its roots, NASCAR took steps to limit the impact of these specially designed models. A new rule for 1970 models required that at least a thousand of a particular design be built, to qualify for the circuit. With mounting public and governmental concern over the environment, and with energy conservation beginning to stir, Detroit started pulling back—and the era of the muscle cars was soon over.

QUALIFYING

When you have a fast race set-up, you'll have a starting point for your qualifying set-up. Don't worry about setting up a car for qualifying until you've come up with a fast, stable chassis for the race.

Many of the concerns that limit what you can do with a race set-up don't apply in qualifying. You're only running a lap or two, so don't be concerned with conserving tires. In fact, you want a set-up that quickly builds heat into the tires, or

Figure 2.12
Load only as much fuel as you need for qualifying.

you'll be sliding all over the track. The real teams use specially designed qualifying engines, but we're stuck with the same tools we used for a race set-up.

SLIPPIN' AND SLIDIN'

Like many aspects of setting up a race car, these factors depend largely on the track and your driving style. But at most tracks, you want a loose set-up for qualifying.

You'll want just enough fuel in the tank for the one or two laps of the qualifying run. When you're running with only a gallon or two, the car's handling characteristics can change drastically. In a race, the car tends to get tighter—develops a push—as it burns through the 22 regulation gallons of fuel. Your race set-up, then, is likely to be much tighter than you're used to. Consult the table at the end of this chapter for the various adjustments to loosen up the car, but we'll take a look at some general pointers here.

GEARING

Starting with your race set-up, shorten fourth gear by two or three steps. On the short tracks, you should be red-lining the tachometer at the end of each straightaway. Even on the super-speedways, you'll want to see that red light flash before you let off the gas. But remember, don't limit your top-end speed by red-lining too far before the end of the straightaway.

SUSPENSION

Softening the rear shocks will move some of the weight to the front end of the car, helping to compensate for the light load in the fuel tank. This should make the car easier to turn and reduce the push condition. Keep the shock at 100% on that pesky left-front wheel, though, to get that tire as hot as possible.

WEIGHT

You can also experiment with weight jacking to give you a faster, looser set-up and fight the push that develops with a low fuel load. Increasing the rear bias and decreasing the wedge should make the rear-end plenty loose.

SPOILERS

If you've already found a comfortable and fast compromise between speed and downforce with your spoilers, you should probably stick with it for the qualifying set-up. It's worth experimenting, though, with a lower rear spoiler to see if you can gain some straightaway speed without losing cornering speed. You don't have to worry about traffic, so you might pick up a tick on the clock if the car will still handle well enough for you to find the line and stick to it.

TIRES

For the tires that run cold—almost always the left-front on an oval—try a hefty decrease in the pressure. That will cause the tire to sag and overheat the outside of the tire's contact patch, but who cares? It'll get hotter, it'll grip better, and you're only asking for a couple of laps out of it.

On the fastest superspeedways—Talladega and Michigan—try overinflating the tires to about 60 pounds. The tires will bulge and overheat in the middle, but it'll give you faster straightaway speed.

YES, MORE PRACTICE

Though you started with a tried-and-true race set-up, all these changes result in a qualifying set-up that bears little resemblance to your race-ready configuration. You don't have to worry about overheating tires, but you still have to keep this beast off the concrete while you try to drive around a track faster than you ever have.

You'll be battling a necessarily loose set-up, so take the time to run several mock qualifying runs to see just how hard you can drive and still keep the car in one piece.

Table 2.1

PROBLEM	TIRES	STAGGER	SHOCKS	LEFT BIAS	REAR BIAS	WEDGE	GEARING	WHEEL LOCK	SPOILERS	DRIVER
Loose or oversteer	Lower rear tire pressure	Decrease			Decrease	Increase			Raise rear spoiler	
Loose exiting turn	Increase left-front tire pressure; lower left-rear		Stiffer left-front shock; softer left-rear shock							
Loose entering turn	Raise right-front tire pressure; lower right-rear		Stiffen right-front shock; soften right-rear							
Pushing or understeer	Lower front tire pressures	Increase	Softer right-front shock		Increase	Decrease			Lower front air dam; Less rear	spoiler
Pushing exiting turn	Lower left-front tire pressure; raise left-rear		Soften left-front shock; stiffen left-rear							
Pushing entering turn	Lower right-front tire pressure; raise right-rear		Softer right-front shock; stiffer right-rear shock							Back off earlier going into turns
Erratic steering								Decrease		
Tire too cool	Decrease air pressure		Stiffer shock							
Tire too hot	Increase air pressure		Softer shock				Slow down			Slow down
Losing grip in turns		Increase		Increase						Slow down
Slow speed on straightaways							Shorter 4th gear		More rear spoiler; reduce air dam	
Slow speed in corners	Increase tire pressures	Increase								
Over-revving on straightaways							Taller 4th gear		Raise rear spoiler	

DRIVING
SCHOOL

[S][O] **YOU'VE SPENT A FEW HOURS IN THE GARAGE, TWEAKING YOUR** racer to come up with a fast, stable set-up. Now for the hard part. The quickest car set-up in the world won't help if you can't do the job behind the wheel.

NASCAR Racing is a blast to play, but it's no Sunday drive. To run with the leaders, you'll have to put in hours of practice. That may sound more like a chore than a game, but this is a simulation that makes you work to win. You didn't think it was gonna be easy, did you? What do you think this is, anyway, a game?

Touring the Track

Think of each track as a different game. There are 16 of these different games in *NASCAR Racing*, and the Track Pack, and each requires a unique strategy and driving style. The approach that made you a hero at Michigan won't mean much next week at North Wilkesboro.

Even so, there are some fundamental guidelines you should keep in mind on the track, whether you're slugging it out at Bristol or sailing around Talladega.

FINDING THE LINE

Forget all the tips, tactics, secrets, and strategies. Until you locate the fast groove around each race track, you'll never run up front. The line differs dramatically from track to track. You need to enter some turns low, some high, and some right in the middle. And the fast groove can change during a race, as your car burns its load of fuel and the tires start to wear out.

The groove is more than a line, it's also a matter of speed. If you enter a turn 10 mph too fast, it won't matter how precisely you hit the groove. You'll slide up the track and out of the groove, and you'll be out of rhythm for the next corner. Check out Chapter 6 to see the ideal speeds at various points on each race track.

Also in Chapter 6, I'll show you the smart strategy and the fast line for each track, but for now let's get the classroom portion of our driving school out of the way.

BOOGIE DOWN THE BLACK RUBBER ROAD

On a real race track, the cars lay down a ribbon of rubber as they run lap after lap on the same part of the track. This dark line marks the fast groove, and you can use it to line up your car to enter and exit the turns.

Note the location of the groove. If the black marks are near the bottom of the track going into a turn, that's where you should be. If the marks start in the middle of the track and sweep down to the bottom in the middle of the turn, then that's the line you should take. The black marks can also serve as reference points for braking going into turns.

Try not to follow those other skid marks—the ones pointing toward the concrete outside wall. These are the monuments to the mistakes of other drivers.

FOLLOW THE LEADERS

If you're having trouble finding the groove, try to learn from your opponents. The computer drivers can be pretty dumb, but they usually know the fast way around the track. During practice—or even during the race—try to keep your car right in the tire tracks of the car in front of you. By following the other car precisely, you might be able to pick up a couple of tenths of a second.

TIP
The blimp view gives you an excellent look at the proper line. Watch where your car is entering and exiting turns, and then watch the computer-controlled cars. Find out where they're gaining ground on you, and you'll probably notice a flaw in your line.

Figure 3.1
Use the blimp view in Replay to zero in on the proper line around a turn.

SEARCHING FOR SPEED

After you get comfortable with both the track and the set-up, and you're running consistent, fast laps, try to experiment with your line to find some more speed.

Alter your entry into turns, higher or lower. Try different entry speeds to see if you can get back on the throttle sooner as you exit a turn. Even if you can't find a faster line, you'll gain experience running on different parts of the race track. You'll have to change your line when passing and running in traffic, so it pays off to get comfortable running *outside* the groove. Check out Chapter 6 for some tips on running different lines on each track.

CORNERING

Usually, the fastest way to get through a turn is to make the curve as straight as possible. Although the exact approach varies from track to track, you should generally enter high-speed turns near the middle of the track, and then ease the car toward the inside as you reach the apex—or center—of the turn. As you begin to accelerate out of the turn, the car's momentum will carry it up the track and toward the outside wall as you head down the straightaway. Run right against the wall as you streak down the straightaway, and then get set up to enter the next turn.

KEEP THE TIRES COOL

I know, you love the sound of squealing tires as you race through the turns. It sounds fast. But if your tires are squealing, that means they're losing grip and sliding across the track. That slows you down and wears out the tires. And it will only get worse. As tire temperatures rise past 225 degrees, they lose grip. And when they lose grip, they slide and get even hotter.

Use tire squeal to help determine the line to take, where to brake, and when to get back on the gas. Try to drive the car just hard enough to be on the *edge* of tire squeal. Here's where pedals can really help, letting you feather the throttle to a point just short of tire squeal.

Sometimes, though, you just can't help it. As you race in heavy traffic, taking different lines to pass, and pushing the car to its limits, you're going to heat up the tires. When that happens, the car will become increasingly difficult to handle. With an overheated right front, the car will tend to "push" up the track coming off a corner. You'll have a tough time steering the car off the wall, and you won't be able to get back on the gas as quickly as you'd like. If you're burning up one of the rear tires, the car will get "loose," with the rear end losing traction and inviting a spin-out.

TIP

The quickest set-ups demand skillful driving. They're usually a bit "loose" and touchy, so if you're still a rookie, you should probably stick to the Ace settings that come with the game. These set-ups are fairly fast, yet stable enough to be forgiving of some driver error. Stick with the Ace set-up until you feel comfortable at a track, then try out the faster set-ups.

The solution is simple: slow down. Just back off a bit and go into the corners at a slower speed. Avoid tire squeal for a few laps and the tire temperatures should begin to fall. Press the F4 key to monitor tire temperatures to see which tire you're abusing. When its temperatures come back to an acceptable level—180 to 225 degrees—then you can pick up the pace again. If tire wear is a real problem, you might want to leave on the temperature display to keep tabs on the tires.

BRAKING MANUALLY

Let's get this out of the way early. If you're driving with the Automatic Braking option on in the Driver Aids menu, turn it off now—at least if you're serious about winning. It's a crutch, and it does nothing but slow you down. You'll never get a true feel for a race track—or how to drive fast on it—with Automatic Braking on.

TIP
Using pedals to control the throttle and brakes can really put you in the driver's seat. Keyboard input forces these critical controls into an on-off mode. No matter how hard or softly you press, either you've got the gas pedal to the floor or you're off the gas completely. Pedals give you graduated control of gas and brakes, and that makes a world of difference in the corners. You can roll out of the throttle going into turns, and then ease back into the gas, feathering the gas through the corner and mashing the pedal to the floor as you head down the straightaway.

So turn it off. Get ready for a frustrating period of adjustment while you learn to drive. But you'll be rewarded quickly with much faster lap times, along with a much better feel for each track. The Automatic Braking is very conservative.

Without it, you'll find you can drive deeper into turns before lifting off the gas, and you'll be able to get back on the throttle sooner. You want proof? My lap speeds at Charlotte jump 8–10 mph without Automatic Braking.

As you zero in on the proper points to begin braking or decelerating, find a reference point on the track or in the grandstands. Smooth, consistent laps are the key to running fast and winning races. After you "dial in" your set-up and find the fast groove, concentrate on getting into a rhythm, getting off the gas and on the brakes at precisely the same points on the track.

If you're comfortable with your hot laps, then you've probably got some speed left in the car. That performance cushion is valuable, since it allows you to crank it up a notch when the race is on the line. When you're running side-by-side with Rusty Wallace with two laps to go at North Wilkesboro, you may have to drive a little deeper into the corner.

GET INTO GEAR

Shifting isn't much of a factor in oval-track racing. Those *&$!)&% road courses, though, are a different matter. We'll take a look at shifting there later in this chapter.

For the oval tracks, shifting is important only for starts and restarts. The gear in which you take the green flag varies, of course, depending on the track and the gear ratios, but you'll usually start off in second or third gear.

You'll want to be turning at least 5,000 rpm so you'll accelerate quickly when you hit the gas. Shift up between 7,000 and 8,000 rpms, getting up to speed as quickly as possible. Get into fourth gear before you reach turn 1, so you won't have to worry about shifting as you negotiate the curve.

There's one exception to oval-track shifting. You'll run faster at Pocono by downshifting to third at times. More on that in Chapter 6.

OUT OF CONTROL

If your set-up is even slightly loose, you'll have to constantly drive your way out of potential spins. This usually happens as

Figure 3.2
At 120 mph on Bristol's high banks, the back end breaks loose. Save it or bite the concrete.

you exit a turn. You know the feeling: the rear end of the car breaks loose and swings out to the right.

Loose set-ups are usually the fastest, but you have to get a feel for driving with them. Obviously, if you have to ease off the throttle coming off the turn, you're losing speed. Remember your high school driving class? Remember Mr. Morton, the shop teacher and driving instructor? How he talked about turning into a spin when you're sliding down hill on an icy road? That's just what you do on the race track. When the back end begins to come around, turn slightly to the right, and then edge back to the left just as the car begins to straighten out.

The timing is critical here. You want the front wheels pointed in the proper direction when the rear tires regain traction. It's *tricky*. If you're steering to the right when the tires catch hold, you're likely to rocket into the concrete wall. Turning too hard in the direction of the spin is called "overcorrecting," and it's probably the most common reason real drivers smack the wall.

Driving a loose car fast through the corners requires constant corrections on the wheel or joystick. You'll probably have to lift off the gas when the car breaks loose, but the faster you correct the spin, the faster you can get back on the throttle. This is driving on the ragged edge, but you'll have to get used to it if you're going to run up front with the champs.

A WEEK AT THE RACES

NASCAR teams spend about 30 weekends a year on the road, crisscrossing the country from New Hampshire to Arizona, from Michigan to Florida. Usually, the teams arrive on the race track on Tuesday or Wednesday for practice, and then they qualify on Thursday or Friday for the race on Sunday. They might get a day off on Monday, and then start the cycle again. It's a tough way to become a scarred-up millionaire, traveling all over the country, doing something you love. You can't get rich playing the game, but at least you get to stay at home.

Don't think of the phases of the race weekend as game options that you can choose from. This game is realistic, so it pays to follow the race events in order: pre-race practice, qualifying, warm-up, and race.

PRACTICE FIRST

It's tempting to ignore practice and jump right into a race. But even if you have a fast set-up and know the track like your own backyard, a few laps of practice will be worth the effort when the green flag falls. You'll get into the rhythm of turning fast laps, so you'll be ready to turn a hot lap in qualifying.

Aside from fine-tuning your set-up and finding the fastest line, use the practice sessions to get comfortable passing and running in traffic. Find another car to run with, and then stick with him. After a few laps, you'll see where you can gain on the other car, and you'll remember where you lose ground. Practice passing at various points on the track, determining the best place to make your move. Don't wait until the green flag drops to learn where to pass.

QUALIFYING

It's tougher than it should be to qualify. You're running on cold tires, and you only have one or two laps to get the car up to full speed. Trouble is, your opponents don't have the same problem, so you've got your work cut out for you. The computer

Figure 3.3
Heavy traffic
makes for a risky
start. Wouldn't
you rather start in
front of this pack?

cars usually qualify at or above their practice speeds, while it's a challenge for you to match your top speed in practice, even with a special qualifying set-up.

And the stakes are big. Starting near the front of the pack is a tremendous advantage when it comes to race day. Banging your way through traffic at 180 mph is exciting, but it's also dangerous. The key to winning is surviving, and it's a lot easier to keep your car in one piece if you're starting on the front row. That way you keep most of the traffic—and the trouble—safely behind you.

GET USED TO THE SET-UP

With a looser set-up and shorter gearing of a qualifying set-up, you'll be carrying more speed into the corners, so get comfortable on the track before you go on the clock. Use the practice session to dial in your line and adjust your driving style to the faster qualifying set-up.

After you've gotten comfortable with your race set-up, load your qualifying set-up and take a hot lap, going for it just as you would when qualifying. Check your speed on the first full lap, which would have been your first lap under the clock in qualifying. Then go back to the pits, reload the set-up, and do it again. You'll be quicker in qualifying.

TIP ▬ ▬ ▬ ▬ ▬ ▬ ▬ ▬ ▬
Tired of qualifying at the back of the field when you have the fastest car in practice? Lower the opponent's strength by two percentage points in the Opponents menu in the Game Options. After qualifying, save and exit the race, and then bump the opponent's strength back to the first setting, whatever it was. In NASCAR jargon, this is known as *cheating*.
▬ ▬ ▬ ▬ ▬ ▬ ▬ ▬ ▬ ▬ ▬ ▬

RUN HARD, RUN DEEP

As you exit the pit road to begin your qualifying run, stand on the throttle as soon as you can so that you'll build some heat into the tires. Go into the first turn hard, sliding the tires. Just be careful that you don't crash before you take the green flag.

Drive deep into the corners, but remember, your exit speed out of a turn is more important. If you're washing out in the turns—pushing up the track—try backing off the gas a little earlier, and then get back into the throttle as quickly as possible.

For most races, you have only one lap to qualify. You'll have your hands full, since the tires are cold and won't stick well. If you get a second lap, it should always be faster than the first. Fortunately, it's your game, so you're always guaranteed a starting spot.

TIP ▬ ▬ ▬ ▬ ▬ ▬ ▬ ▬ ▬
If you screw up on your qualifying lap, hit Escape and try again. It's cheating, of course, but you can do this as many times as you like until you make a good run.
▬ ▬ ▬ ▬ ▬ ▬ ▬ ▬ ▬ ▬ ▬ ▬

Because racing in traffic is so difficult, you should consider starting at the back of the pack while you're learning. It's easy to crash when you're racing with packs of car in front and behind you. By starting at the rear, you'll have time to get into a rhythm and heat up your tires, without worrying about avoiding other cars.

RACE STRATEGY

Your strategic approach to a race is determined in large part by the length of the event. Whatever the strategy, keep it in mind as soon as the green flag falls. You may not be able to drive as fast or as consistently as the computer cars on some tracks, but you can always outsmart them.

SPRINTS

No pacing yourself here. If you're running a short race—one in which you won't have to pit for gas or tires—you can throw out the strategy and charge for the front. You want to keep all four wheels on the track, but you can't afford to lie back, either.

WARNING If you're starting toward the back of the pack, take it easy on the first lap or so. As the cars bunch up in front of you, they tend to slow down through the turns. If you're running at full speed, you might smash into them before you know what happened. This is more of a problem on the short tracks and the road courses, so be ready to lift off the throttle and maybe tap the brakes. If you're good, though, you can pass a few cars when they get caught in this bottleneck.

THE LONG HAUL

Longer races—more than 100 miles—present a different racing challenge. You're not going to win the race in the first few laps, so you can take more time working your way to the front.

This is *real racing*, with strategy and pit stops often determining the winner. You don't have to push the car to its limits all the time. Use your head, time your pit stops wisely, and you can get to the head of the field without abusing your car.

THE RHYTHM METHOD

Your goal, of course, is to run fast laps—and consistent ones. If your lap speeds vary by more than a few tenths of a second per lap, you're probably losing ground over the long haul. Your goal is to run smooth, comfortable laps.

Turning consistent laps requires intense concentration as you try to get into the rhythm of braking and accelerating at precise points on the race track. The longer you run, the smoother your laps should be.

Don't save and exit a race unless it's absolutely necessary. Restarting a race cold is always tough; you're asking for disaster. Don't even Pause the race unless you really need a break. You'll break your concentration and put yourself in a dangerous position when you restart.

TIP

When you have to Pause a race, wait until you're at the front end of a straightaway and clear of traffic. If you must exit and save a race, go to Preseason Practice and run a few laps on that track to get back into the rhythm before restarting the race.

RUSH-HOUR TRAFFIC

Negotiating traffic is one of the most difficult challenges in *NASCAR Racing*, but if you handle it well you can turn it into an advantage over the competition.

The computer cars don't handle traffic very well, so you can usually catch the leaders—even if they're faster—when they start working through the slower lapped traffic.

Lapped cars—at least the computer-controlled ones—usually move over slightly to give you room to pass. Some won't be so cooperative, depending on their aggressiveness rating. Don't force the issue too quickly. Bide your time until you get a clean shot to pass, unless you're desperately running for the win late in a race.

THE LEAD LAP

In *NASCAR Racing*, each car's laps are tallied. If the leader comes around the track and passes you, you're a lap down— you've run one lap fewer than the leader. If the caution flag comes out, you're in trouble. The cars on the lead lap can pit on the first lap after taking the yellow flag, but cars one or more laps down have to wait until the second lap. That means you have to restart the race behind every car on the lead lap, not just the leader who passed you.

When you get lapped, your priority shifts from winning the race to a more immediate goal—getting back on the same lap with the leaders. There are two ways of doing this: passing the leader under race conditions, or trying to stretch your fuel and tires so that you pit well after the rest of the field.

There's no secret to getting your lap back under green. You have to chase down and pass the leader. First, you have to find out who's leading the race. You can Pause and check the standings, or use the ( ]) key to scroll to the top of the in-car standings display. The leader is your target. You can use Replay to find out where he is on the track. If you can chase him down and catch him in traffic, you can pass him and get back on the lead lap. Then, if a caution comes out, you'll be able to circle the track and fall in behind the lead pack.

Your best bet for regaining your lost lap might be through well-timed pit stops. If the race stays under green for a long period, stretch your fuel and tires as far as they will go. The computer cars are pretty conservative; they'll usually stop a

Figure 3.4
The two-abreast start: the most dangerous moment in the race.

few laps before they absolutely must. If you can stay out on the track while the leaders pit, you'll get your lap back. Now just pray for a caution flag while you're ahead of the leader.

TIP   If you have no scruples at all, you can sometimes save and exit your way out of trouble. If the leader is closing in on you and threatening to put you a lap down, exit from the race and save it. When you restart, you'll be under a caution flag and back in the main pack. But can you live with yourself after such a low-down trick? My advice: don't do it. It's only a game.

SURVIVING THE START

When the green flag drops, 30 or 40 cars running side-by-side and bumper-to-bumper go screaming into turn 1, on cold tires and just inches apart. Good luck.

Unless it's a two- or three-lap dash to the checkered flag, take it easy when the green flag flies. On most tracks you'll have to tiptoe through the first couple of turns, so be prepared to get passed. The most important rule: hold your line. Wild swings on the joystick or wheel are a recipe for a wreck. Keep it steady and straight. After you've survived the first couple of turns, you can settle into your groove and start racing.

Cold tires don't bother the computer cars too much. They're a bit slower in the first couple of laps, but they're darned good at running on cold tires. Be prepared to lose a couple of positions on the start—or a restart. Be patient and don't panic.

GET IN LINE
At most tracks, the inside groove is the preferred line, so get down there as quickly—and safely—as you can. If you're starting on the inside, hold that line. If you're starting on the outside row, look for an opening to get to the bottom of the track. When the left-side mirror is clear, move over to get into the inside groove. Racing into a turn with a car on your inside—especially on cold tires—can end your race in a hurry.

RESTARTS

While restarts are exciting and challenging, they're not the nightmare that the start of the race can be. After caution periods, the field lines up in single file for the restart. Strategy varies, depending on where you are in the field, though restarts are a lot less harrowing than the two-abreast start.

The computer cars probably will still be able to corner faster than you during the first lap, but you should be able to keep cars behind you by holding the preferred line. But take it easy, because if you go into a turn too fast and your car slips out of the groove, somebody will jump alongside you.

JUMPING THE FLAG
Technically, you aren't supposed to hit the gas until the green flag waves. By anticipating the flag by a couple of heartbeats, though, you can get a jump on your opponents. Just be sure

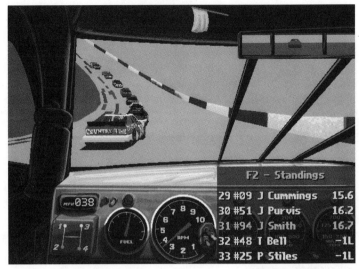

Figure 3.5
Be quick with the throttle and you can get past several of those cars before you get to turn 1.

you don't pass anybody—*including* the pace car—before the flag waves.

This trick works best on single-file restarts, and the outside is usually the best place to pass. Line up slightly to the outside of the car in front, and then floor it when the pace car turns left for pit road. The cars in front will usually bunch up on the restart, allowing you to pass several cars down the front stretch. Try to get back into line before you reach turn 1, though, or you're likely to lose all the positions you've gained, and maybe a few more.

STAYING ALIVE

Wrecks happen, and guess what? Sometimes you don't cause them. Computer cars crash in basically one fashion: they break loose, go up the track, and slap the outside wall. That simple wreck can turn into a flaming melee, though, as other cars swerve and brake to avoid the sliding car.

Some wrecks are unavoidable: a car slides out of control and collects several other racers, blocking the track in front of you. Crashes happen quickly, so be prepared to dodge. Watch

Figure 3.6
Trouble ahead!
Say a quick
prayer and look
for open track.

as far ahead as you can. When you see smoke, get off the gas
and head for clear track. Cars that hit the outside wall generally stay there, but sometimes they'll slide down the track and
into your path.

LIMPING HOME

When you do wreck (and it's pretty often, huh, Bubba?), get
the car straightened out and moving as fast as you can. But
don't be reckless. If there's a line of cars screaming past as you
sit against the wall, let 'em go. Pull into oncoming traffic and
you'll put the finishing touches on your wreck. Wait for an
opening, and then head for the pits if necessary.

If your car has sustained wheel damage, you'll have to pit.
With serious wheel damage, your car can be difficult to drive.
Sometimes, you'll roll to a stop and be unable to get the car
moving again. There's no wrecker to pick you up, so you're
through for the day. Just hit Escape, walk back to the pits, and
prepare for your interview with Ned Jarrett. "Well, Ned, the
tire blowed and we hit the wall. But the Interstate Batteries
Champion Spark Plug Tide All-Pro Auto Parts Goodyear
Valvoline Ford Thunderbird was really runnin' good. We'll get
'em next week."

Figure 3.7
Sorry, Junior.
You're done
for the day.

YELLOW FLAG FEVER

The rules state that cars race back to the finish line when a caution flag flies. But the yellow flag means that somebody has crashed, so racing at full speed around the track can be hazardous to your health. Try to keep up your speed, but keep your attention focused as far ahead on the track as you can. It's easy to plow right into a group of wrecked cars. So take it easy. You might lose a couple of spots getting through the wreck, but at least you'll be able to restart the race.

PASSING

Each track has different lines, and therefore different places to pass. We'll look at each track in depth in Chapter 6, but for now, here are a few general tips to keep in mind as you work your way through traffic.

THE STRAIGHTAWAY

If you've got better top speed than the competition, then the straightaway is the safest place to pass. As you go through a turn, stay as close as possible to the rear bumper of the car in front of you. Be careful not to run up on the other car so fast that you have to lift off the gas as you exit the turn. Time your approach so that you're closing on the other car as you come

Figure 3.8
An inside pass in the dogleg will beat that guy into turn 1 at Charlotte.

off the turn, and then dive to the inside or outside, depending on the track. When you clear the car, you'll see it in the center section of your rear-view mirror. Now get into position to the enter the turn properly.

As you make a pass running down the straightaway, you're likely to be carrying more speed as you approach the next turn, so be prepared. Touch the brakes or back off the gas a bit to make sure you're in position to take the proper line—usually low—through the turn. Even if the other car is now running faster, you should be able to hold him off if you stay in the racing groove.

PASSING IN THE TURNS
On most of the short tracks, the straightaways are too short to depend on sheer speed to make your passes. You'll have to make your moves in the corners. The inside groove is almost always the preferred line on the short tracks, so you'll have to take that line away from the car in front in order to get by.

Run as close as you can to the car in front. If you bump him a bit, well, that's just racin'. If you can muster enough straight-away speed, try to get alongside the car on the inside as you head toward the next turn. You have the preferred line, so you should be able to take the position. Just drive a smooth, nor-mal line through the corner, and the guy on the outside will

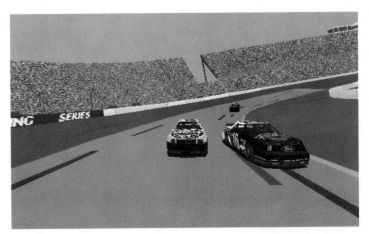

Figure 3.9
On the short tracks, the car on the inside usually wins the battle for position.

usually have to back off and let you have the spot. Be careful, though, not to go into the turn too hard, or you'll slide up the track and collide with the car beside you.

THE OUTSIDE PASS

You can pass cars to the outside at several tracks, and in a few cases an outside pass is the better choice. More on that in Chapter 6. If you're beating a car coming off a turn—and he's got the inside line locked up—then try to get outside of him as you exit the corner. Ideally, you'll get past and be able to move down in front of the other car before you get to the next turn.

Passing on the outside in a turn requires skill and a bit of nerve, as well as a feel for how close you are to the other car. Cut down too low in the turn and you'll bang into the car on the inside. But if you go too high in the turn, you'll lose both speed and the position. Stay as low as you can, without bumping the other car. This takes practice, but remember: you can usually run lower than you think. After trying an outside pass, check out the replay to see how much room you had between the cars.

DEFENSIVE DRIVING

The computer-controlled cars are tough to pass, but they're pretty easy to hold off, as long as you stay in the groove. Even if

Figure 3.10
At Darlington,
you'd better get
used to running
high on the track,
and passing
even higher.

the cars behind you are clearly faster than you, if you don't move out of the racing line, they'll have a hard time getting around.

Stray out of the groove, however, and the car behind you will move quickly to take advantage. When another driver gets beside you, let the situation dictate how you react. If you're sliding out of control, let him go and concentrate on getting the car back under control and back in line. If your car's holding a stable line, then decide if you want to try to hold off the other car. Do you want to go into the next turn side-by-side, probably on the outside? Maybe not.

Remember where you are in the race. If you have 300 laps to go, you may want to let the other guy go, instead of risking a crash. Of course, if you just got the white flag, go for it.

CAUGHT OUT OF THE GROOVE
Many times, you have more to worry about than one car behind you. The racing here is close, with several cars usually running bumper-to-bumper. So if one car gets alongside you, there's often somebody right behind, ready to follow him through.

When you're caught out of the groove in heavy traffic, a line of cars just might blow past you like a freight train. There's usually not much to be done, short of making a dumb move and triggering a multicar crash. Just bite the bullet and let 'em

Figure 3.11
When you get caught out of the draft, you might lose several positions before you can get back in line.

go. Watch your mirror for a break in traffic, and get back in line as soon as possible.

KEEP AN EYE ON THE MIRROR

When you're running in heavy traffic, the rear-view mirror is your best friend. Use it well, and you can hold off Dale Earnhardt himself.

The mirror is divided into three parts. The center section shows you what is directly behind your car. The left- and right-hand sections show the areas to the left and right of the car. That sounds obvious, but the three-way mirror is a valuable tool.

As a car running behind you moves its nose alongside your rear bumper on the inside, you'll see its front bumper edge into the left section of the mirror. If you dive left now, there's gonna be a crash. Likewise, as you pass a car on the inside, you'll see your opponent move from the right side of the mirror to the center section. When the right side is clear, you've made the pass, and you can now move in front of him if necessary.

WHERE THE RUBBER MEETS THE ROAD

Tires are the single most important factor in going fast. In the garage, as we saw in Chapter 2, chassis set-up revolves around

Figure 3.12
Better not cut
left with that car
on the inside!
Watch the mirror
until you're sure
it's clear.

tire temperatures. On the track, tire wear determines your speed, how aggressively you can drive, and how many pit stops you'll have to make.

If you've developed a good set-up for a track and turned plenty of practice laps, you'll know whether tire wear is going to be a problem during the race. The right front is usually the culprit, since weight shifts to that corner as the car goes through a corner.

TAMING THE TRACKS

Each type of track demands a different approach, but let's look at some overall strategies for the general categories of tracks You'll find a detailed discussion of tactics and strategy for each track in Chapter 6.

SHORT TRACKS

Running bumper-to-bumper at 200 mph is thrilling, but it's the short tracks that represent what NASCAR's root: beating and

Figure 3.13
The action is tight and furious on the short tracks. Here, survival is the key.

banging with 30 cars on a li'l ol' half-mile track, having the guts to push your car just a little harder and further into the corner than the guy beside you.

TIP

If you're just beginning your racing career, focus on a single track until you get the feel for what it takes to run smooth, fast laps. While you experiment with different keyboard commands, joysticks, and wheels, you'll also be getting familiar with a single track. Atlanta is a good choice for rookies. It's fast, smooth, and wide, and it has more than one passing lane. More importantly, it's fairly easy to drive, yet you can't run flat-out all the way around. This 1.5-mile track is an ideal learning ground for budding NASCAR stars.

RACE STRATEGY

The short tracks—less than ¾ mile—are marked by close-quarters racing on a tight, often narrow, racing surface. This is white-knuckle, heart-skipping racing at its best.

Winning—and surviving—a 300- or 400-mile race at Martinsville is no easy task. Talladega's like a drive down the interstate compared to waging war at Martinsville, Bristol, or North Wilkesboro.

You spend most of the time cornering in heavy traffic, so the demands on your concentration are enormous. Tight turns are a test of your driving skill, though, so you can make up ground in a hurry.

Even if your car's not especially fast, you can usually *drive* your way to the front of the pack on the short tracks—*if* you're good enough.

And while you shouldn't be too aggressive, you need to keep a steady pace with the leaders, even if you're running in the middle of the pack. It's easy to get lapped on these short tracks.

QUALIFYING

Pay special attention to your qualifying set-up on the short tracks. You always want to start as close to the front as you can, but it's *critical* on the half-mile tracks, where tight traffic and frequent crashes make survival a challenge.

PASSING

Above all, be patient. When another car gets alongside you on a short track, it's often smart to let him pass. Unless it's late in the race or you're trying to stay on the lead lap, running side-by-side into a tight corner is probably not worth the risk. When you're trying to get around somebody, take your time. Eventually, the other driver will make a slip and slide up the race track and out of the groove. Then you can pass without changing your line.

Of course, some drivers don't want to give up their position, so a little friendly tap on the bumper might get their attention—and might knock them up out of the groove. Be careful, though, not to smash in your front grill.

INTERMEDIATE TRACKS

These tracks are a mixed bag. You get the wide, smooth surface and sweeping turns of 2-mile Michigan to the tight,

Figure 3.14
Most mid-size tracks give you a little more room to relax when the field gets stretched out.

one-groove track at the 1-mile Dover speedway—and just about everything in between.

RACE STRATEGY

Expect tight racing for the first few laps after a green flag, but the field tends to get "strung out" more on the longer tracks. Packs of five or six cars often run several seconds apart, so you'll find yourself climbing through the field one pack at a time.

The speeds are much faster on these tracks, but you still can't go flat-out through the turns).

Because there are typically fewer caution periods on the longer tracks, you can win or lose just on the timing of pit stops. Stretch your fuel and tires as far as you can under green-flag conditions.

QUALIFYING

Starting close to the front isn't as critical here as it is on the short tracks, but it's always nice to see clear track in front of you.

PASSING

Long straightaways make for relatively easy passing, so you can work your way to the front fairly quickly. The exceptions are Rockingham, Dover, and Richmond, where passing is always a challenge.

Figure 3.15
Hope you don't
have too many
cars to pass on
this road course!

TALLADEGA

This 2.66-mile superspeedway is pure speed. Chassis set-up
and drafting skill will win for you here. There's only one track
like it in the game. See Chapter 6 for the winning strategy.

ROAD COURSES

Let's face it: everything about racing on the road courses is difficult—braking, passing, even running consistent laps. These
long, twisting tracks are the ultimate test of your driving ability.

It's like the NASCAR drivers say: slow down to go faster
on the road courses. That sounds illogical, but it really works.
The most common mistake drivers make on road courses is
entering a turn too fast. That throws your car off line and keeps
you from getting back on the gas as quickly as you could. That
robs you of speed on the next straightaway. Slower entries and
faster exits will mean quicker lap times.

The road courses present another challenge: constant shifting. Although you might prefer to leave the Automatic Shifting
option on while you learn the tracks, you'll eventually go much
faster if you do the shifting yourself.

Use the gears in conjunction with the brakes to slow down
to enter a turn. Downshift to the appropriate gear, and then get

on the brakes as you approach the turn. This takes a lot of seat time to master, so be patient.

> **TIP**
>
> Give yourself a break on the road courses and turn on Automatic Shifting and Braking Help in the Options menu, at least until you learn the tracks. These driving aids are a bad habit to get into on the oval tracks, but on the more difficult road courses they can save you a lot of frustration while you're learning. Not having to worry about shifting is especially helpful, letting you concentrate on the track ahead. As soon as you get comfortable on the course, though, turn off the driving aids. Once you get the hang of it, you'll go much faster doing the shifting and braking yourself.

QUALIFYING

Nowhere is qualifying as important as it is on the road courses. Since passing is so tough, it's hard to finish well ahead of where you start, unless you get lucky with cautions and pit stops. Trouble is, it's also harder to qualify well on the road courses. The computer drivers are aces on these tracks.

PASSING

Except for the rare long straightaway, almost all passing on road courses is accomplished by outbraking the other car to get on the inside going into a tight turn. That means driving into the turn deeper than the other guy, then getting on the brakes hard.

THE COMPETITORS

Unless you're racing against a friend via modem, or against the aces on Papyrus's multi-player service, then you're up against just a bunch of robots. It may seem like that guy in the black #3 is really The Intimidator, but he's only obeying the instructions of the programmer.

I'll show you how to adjust the strength and behavior of the computer-controlled cars in Chapter 7. For now, let's take a look at how they behave on the track.

HOW THEY PASS

As noted earlier, you can usually hold off a faster competitor if you claim the fast groove and stick to it precisely. That's easier said than done, of course, and if you slip slightly a fast car will immediately move to get beside you.

The computer drivers are best at passing under braking, as they enter a turn. That tendency makes them more aggressive—and tougher to outrun—on the short tracks and on the road courses.

On the medium-length tracks, the computer drivers are less of a threat to pass, as long as you're fast and running in their groove. Because they usually try to pass under braking, they won't often pull out to pass on the straightaway.

Once again, Talladega is unique. Computer drivers at this superspeedway are more aggressive in Version 1.2, but they still tend to follow along in the draft, then fall back as they negotiate traffic. Except for the start of the race, you should be able to hold off the computer drivers for hours at a time at Talladega.

HOW TO PASS THEM

The limitations of artificial intelligence make it pretty easy to predict the behavior of the computer drivers, and that should help you plot your strategy to get around them.

Unless they're trying to pass or to maneuver through slower traffic, the computer drivers will stick to a single fast groove around the track. That focus on taking the right line is what makes them so darned fast on the road courses—and it's what makes them vulnerable to your human cunning and ability to make split-second decisions.

When computer drivers approach slower traffic that is occupying the groove, they'll usually back off a bit as they wait for the lane to clear. This is your chance. If you're close at all, you can often dive for an open bit of track and pass the whole bunch of them.

Without the benefit of race traffic, it's often best to just follow the lead car until it slips out of the groove, giving you the opportunity to drive up on the inside.

Watch out, though. Some drivers are much more likely to cut down the track to block the pass. Now you can check your aggressiveness rating. Here's a general approach: if you've pulled even with the lead car, go for it; if you just have your front bumper alongside the rear of the other guy, you might want to back off to avoid the crash.

THE PITS

IT **SOUNDS LIKE A TIRED SAYING IN AUTO RACING, BUT IT'S TRUE:** *races are won and lost in the pits.* You can blow past the entire field on the track, then screw up on a pit stop and lose all the track positions you've gained. Consider this: at 200 mph at Talladega, every second you spend sitting in the pits will cost you about 300 yards on the track.

You don't want a bum pit stop to cost you a hard-fought victory, so plan your pit strategy carefully before the green flag falls. Make sure you know when to pit, how to pit, and what to do when you get there.

Pit Strategy

Even if you can't beat your opponents on the track, you can often outsmart them in the pits. We'll take a closer look at pit strategy for each track in Chapter 6, but as a general rule, you'll want to stretch fuel and tires as far as you can, while limiting your stops to the yellow flags whenever possible.

With smart pit strategy, you can turn a middle-of-the-pack performance into a victory, or turn a last-place run into a top-10 finish.

PLOT YOUR STOPS

As you prepare for a race, plan your pit stops on the assumption that the race will run under the green flag from start to finish. The race almost certainly won't go green all the way, but you should be ready for the possibility. Refer to the data on fuel mileage and tire wear for the various tracks in Chapter 6 to see which factor is going to force you to stop. Then calculate how many stops you'll need to run the full race.

If the race runs without a caution—or maybe with just one or two caution periods—your calculations might pay off a bit, allowing you to run the event on one fewer stop than your competitors.

Fuel: 12.0 gal
Mileage: 3.86 mpg
Proj Laps: 89
Fill To: 22 gal

Figure 4.1
Be prepared to calculate fuel mileage at any time when the yellow flag flies.

THE MILEAGE RACE

As you practice for a race, check your miles-per-gallon reading with the F3 key at the end of the longest straightaway. Use that figure to calculate how much fuel you'll need to run the entire race, and then see how many fuel stops you have to make. Running out of gas is disastrous, so be careful to build some cushion into your calculations.

For example, suppose you're running a 300-mile race at Talladega. Near the end of the backstretch, your fuel reading shows you're getting 6.2 miles per gallon. Let's say an even 6, just to be safe. That means you can go about 132 miles on a full 22-gallon tank. Round up the track's 2.66-mile length to 2.7, then divide into 132. That gives you 48.9 laps, so you can figure 49 laps per tank of fuel.

The projected-laps figure on your fuel display gives you the same number, but you should get used to calculating it on your own. That way, if you want to take on a partial fuel load—just enough to finish—late in a race, you'll be ready.

For instance, you're forced to pit for fuel with 16 laps to go, green-flag stop. Your tires will go the distance, so you want to stop just long enough to get enough gas to finish. Sixteen laps times 2.7 miles equals 43.2 miles. At six miles per gallon, eight gallons of fuel will get you to the finish line with a bit to spare. The few seconds you'll save in the pits might gain you several positions on the track—and maybe even give you the win.

Of course, with tires that are wearing quickly, you'll have to change your strategy. If your tires aren't lasting a full fuel stop, tire wear will dicate your pit strategy.

TIP

If you'd rather play it safe, then just follow the leader, pitting whenever he does to stay in the same sequence. You won't win on pit strategy this way, but you won't lose the race in the pits, either.

TIMING IS EVERYTHING

Let your position on the track dictate when you make a pit stop. If you're leading, don't let the other cars determine whether you stop. For instance, if you're under a caution flag and you've figured you need two more stops to finish the race—whether you stop now or not—then you should stay on the track. If the cars behind you stop, ignore 'em. They, too, will have to stop twice more, so they've gained nothing.

If, in the same situation as above, you're in the middle of the pack when other cars pit, you'll pass those cars when they stop, and you'll still be on the same pit-stop schedule.

Under green flag conditions, stretch your fuel and tires as far as you can. You might get lucky and catch a caution after other cars have stopped during the green flag. This can put you a lap up on the field, especially on a short track.

Figure 4.2
Be careful not to pass anyone as you head down pit road. That's a penalty, and you will be caught.

GREEN FLAG STOPS

The strategy for pitting under green-flag conditions is simple: don't stop until you have to. Be careful, though: if you run out of gas and can't coast back to the pits, your race is over.

As you approach the end of your green-flag run—determined either by fuel or tires—focus your attention on that limiting factor. If you'll run out of fuel before a tire wears out and blows, press F3 to monitor remaining fuel. When you're down to two gallons—maybe one gallon on a short track—head for the pit road. If it's tires you're worried about, press F5 and keep an eye on tire wear. Pit when there's just a speck of red left on the tire display.

Getting the most out of your green-flag runs gives you two advantages. You may catch a caution after everybody else has stopped under green. And by stretching your runs throughout the race, you might be able to go the distance on one fewer stop than your competitors.

WARNING When your tires screech, you're wearing 'em out. If you're trying to go as far on a green-flag run as you can, back off a bit to save your tires.

STOPPING UNDER THE YELLOW

Of course, when the yellow flag flies, all your carefully planned pit strategy usually goes out the window. Each time the caution comes out, you have a decision to make, one that might determine—even early in the race—whether you win or lose. The decision whether to pit depends on a number of factors: track position, the fuel and tire situation, and the number of laps remaining.

WHEN TO PIT

Unless you're just a few laps into a green-flag run, you'll probably want to take advantage of a yellow flag to pit for tires and gas. That's not a law, since so many other factors come into play. As a general rule, if you've burned more than 25% of your fuel load when the yellow flag flies, think seriously about pitting.

If you're near the back of the field, or one of the last cars on your lap, you might as well come in to "top off" the gas tank during a caution, no matter how little fuel you've burned. The extra gas will allow you to go a few laps farther during the next green-flag run than the other cars, and that just might give you an advantage.

WHEN TO STAY OUT

Not pitting under the yellow flag is usually a gamble. Unless you pitted earlier, when the other cars stayed out, this is a risky call. You might pass the entire field by not pitting, but if you're forced to pit later under green-flag racing, you're in trouble.

Consider tire wear, how many cars are on your lap, how many laps are left in the race, and where you are in the standings. If you're at a track where there are typically few cautions, such as Pocono, you'd better pit while you can. At Bristol, where there's often a caution every few laps, not pitting might pay off. You'll find more detailed discussion of pit strategy for specific tracks in Chapter 6.

TIP If you're running for points and aren't likely to lead the race under racing conditions, stay out during the first lap of a yellow-flag pit stop. You might be able to lead the next caution lap, and pick up five bonus points in the championship race. I know, it's just five points, but that's the way Jeff, Dale, and Rusty do it.

STARTING FRESH

When you go back out on the track, recalculate your pit stops for the rest of the race. Assume the race will run green the rest of the way, just as you did before the start.

Always think about how much fuel you'll need to finish the race. When a caution comes out, check your mileage and calculate how much fuel you need to finish. A gallon or two of fuel might put you within reach of the finish—without having to stop again.

TALKING TO THE CREW

The real NASCAR teams use two-way radios to discuss strategy and plan pit stops, but you're stuck with a text display, sort of a throwback to the old hand-held pit boards. The display shows you what the pit crew will do to the car when you stop, usually four new tires and a full load of fuel.

Hit the Pause key when you're ready to pit, whether it's going to be a caution or a green-flag stop. Press the F9 key to access pit communications. Make sure the display matches what you want done on this stop. Your options are: how many tires to change, how much gas to load, and whether to repair damage. You can also make adjustment to three areas of the car set-up: cross-weight, tire pressure, and the rear spoiler.

Figure 4.3
"Since an encounter with the concrete destroyed the right-front tire, I guess I'd better get a new one. But with only five laps to go, there's no need to change the left-side tires."

TWO TIRES OR FOUR?

It's usually wise to take on four tires, especially during caution periods. But there may be a situation where you can get by on just two tires. Pay attention to tire wear and see if tires on one side of the car are wearing much better than those on the other side. The right-side tires usually wear faster, since they're taking most of the abuse in the corners on an oval track.

If the left-side tires aren't very worn, consider getting new right-side tires only, especially if you have to make a green-flag stop. You may gain several positions, assuming other cars are pitting. Just don't forget about those older tires, because they almost certainly won't last a full fuel run.

GAS AND GO

Don't take on four tires and 22 gallons of gas if you don't have to. If you must stop for fuel in the closing laps of a race, get only what you need to finish. Pause the race while you plan your last stop. Calculate how much fuel you need to finish, allowing some room for error.

Check the tires and see if they can go the distance. This is more of a guess. If your tires have been wearing out before you need fuel on previous green-flag runs, then you're probably going to have to take on some more tires. To save precious seconds in the pits, get only the tires you need to finish.

TWEAKING THE SET-UP

Adjustments to the car are limited during the race to the cross-weight, the rear spoiler, and tire pressure. With an established and comfortable set-up, this shouldn't be necessary. But if your car is handling so poorly that you just can't keep up with other cars, you might as well try an adjustment. Don't order radical changes. You might go back on the track in a car that's impossible to drive.

See Chapter 2 for a more detailed explanation of these adjustments.

CROSS-WEIGHT

Adjusting cross-weight, or wedge, is perhaps the most important mid-race adjustment you can make. By shifting the angle at which the chassis rides on the springs, you can change how weight shifts to the four tires as the car goes through the corner.

In the real world, a crew member makes wedge adjustments by turning a bolt located at the right rear and left rear of the car.

If the car is chronically loose—the back end tends to lose traction—you can correct this oversteer by increasing cross weight. For a car that's experiencing understeer—pushing in the corners and refusing to turn left—reduce the cross-weight. Whichever way you go, try to limit wedge adjustments to two or three pounds at a time.

REAR SPOILER

Bumping the rear spoiler up or down a bit affects the flow of air over the rear of car. During a race, NASCAR crews use cutting-edge technology to make this adjustment—they use a trusty hammer. If you're getting badly outrun down the straight-aways, you might consider telling the crew to lower the spoiler angle by 1 or 2 degrees. If you're fast on the straightaways but getting killed in the corners, consider bumping the spoiler up a bit to create more downforce and better traction.

Spoiler adjustments usually are an alternative only on the longer tracks—1.5 miles or more. On the short tracks and road courses, the spoiler is generally set as high as possible.

Though you can change this setting during the race, you should have this part of your car set-up tuned in well before the green flag flies. Mid-race spoiler adjustment should be very rare.

TIRE PRESSURE

By making a slight adjustment to tire pressure, you may be able to lower the temperature of an overheated tire. If you have a tire that's getting hot and losing grip, increase the pressure in that tire by a couple of degrees and see what happens during the next run.

You may also be able to help cure oversteer or understeer through adjustment to tire pressure. If the rear tires are losing traction—oversteer—try increasing the pressure slightly on the rear tires. Doing the same to the front tires might help an understeer problem.

GETTING IN AND OUT

It ought to be a short respite from the gut-wrenching intensity of close-quarter racing, but the pit stops can be just as nerve-wracking as the racing on the track. Entering and exiting the pit road—especially during the mad rush to the pits under a caution flag— can be as dangerous as the start of the race.

UNDER GREEN

Getting into the pits safely is the greatest challenge here. After calculating your fuel mileage and tire wear, decide on what lap you're going to pit. Try not to make a rash decision on pitting— you'll have to go through a series of precise maneuvers to get in and out of the pits quickly.

Figure 4.4
Just getting off the track is a dangerous maneuver in heavy traffic.

It's easy to crash when you're slowing down and dropping off the banking onto the flat apron of the track. So take it easy, especially if you haven't made very many stops under green on a particular track. Depending on the track, you'll want to start slowing down in turn 4, while you're still on the track. As you exit the turn, drop down to the apron, continuing to slow. Use the gears, downshifting to help you slow the car as you approach your pit.

You don't want to crash trying to pit, but neither do you want to waste a lot of time getting onto the pit road. The performance of your pit crew is out of your control. The variable is how quickly you can get to the pits. If you come back onto the track after a series of green-flag stops and find you've lost ground to the leaders, you've nobody to blame but yourself.

With some practice, you'll learn how quickly you can get the car slowed down to enter the pits. Just take it easy until you feel confident about fast pit-road entrances.

Race traffic can play a role when you're deciding when to pit. If you're in the middle of a pack of cars when you're due to pit, see if you have enough fuel and tires left to go a couple more laps. You might get run over if you slow down to enter the pits in heavy traffic. Either get past the traffic or let it go by, leaving you some room to get into the pits.

Figure 4.5
During yellow flags, pit road can be more risky than the freeway during rush hour.

TIP
Use the pre-race practice sessions to get a feel for slowing your speed, getting off the racing surface, and entering the pits. You don't want to try your first green-flag stop when you're leading late in the race.

UNDER YELLOW

Green-flag stops can be scary, but it's usually the yellow-flag stops that are the most dangerous. Every car on the lead lap may pit on the lap after the field takes the caution flag, and they usually do. That means 30 or more cars crowding "pit row."

This is pure chaos, and the other drivers sometimes seem determined to crash into you as you try to get to your pit space.

As cars circle the track under the caution, the computer cars that intend to pit will line up to the inside. Stay as close as possible to the car in front of you, and stay as far left as you can, to prevent another pitting car from getting to the left of you and causing a wreck as you head for the pits.

Your crew is waiting in the first pit space, just past the entrance to the pit road. In real racing, that's considered a disadvantage. In real NASCAR racing, the points champion from the previous year gets to pick his space, and they usually choose the last one—all the way down at the end of the pit road. In this game, where you're running in the pack determines whether your spot is a safe one or an invitation to disaster. If you're in the back, the pit road should be clear when you leave your pit.

But if you're the first car into the pits, you'll have to negotiate heavy traffic as you leave. That's when it can get hairy, as cars pull out of their pits and jockey for position getting back out on the track.

WARNING — — — — — — — — — Pull your car as straight as possible into your pit space, especially when you have lots of cars behind you. If you park at an angle—with your rear end jutting into the entrance lane—you might get slammed by another car. Your car will be damaged, and you'll be angry.

The pit road actually has three lanes: the line of pit stalls, and then two lanes to the right for cars entering and exiting. The computer cars use the middle lane—just to the right of the pit spaces—to accelerate in and out of their stalls and merge into traffic in the far right lane. As you leave the pits, keep your car in the far-right lane. Unfortunately, that's not enough to keep you safe from some of these guys. Watch as other cars leave their pits, and be ready to dodge if they pull out in front of you.

FINDING YOUR PIT

Make sure you know exactly where you need to stop the car. There's a pretty precise spot, and if you're off the mark, your

Figure 4.6
Stop the car when the pit sign is positioned at the top of the windshield.

crew will just stand there, waiting. Use the red "Pit" sign held by a crew member as your mark. Stop so that the sign is just at the top of your windshield, with maybe the top portion of the sign out of your view.

If you overshoot your pit, you'll have to back up. Stop short and you'll have to creep up until you hit the right spot. Either way, you've lost some valuable seconds to the other drivers. The computer-controlled cars don't make dumb mistakes. That's left up to us humans.

THE DREADED BLACK FLAG

When you see this flag, it means you've done something stupid and you're in trouble with the NASCAR officials. This consultation flag requires you to report to your pits for a stop-and-go penalty. It can be devastating to your chances of winning the race.

The penalty is steep. You won't know you've been caught until you cross the starting line to take the green flag. Then you'll be black-flagged.

Figure 4.7
"Hey buddy, where's the fire?" It's back to the pits for a stop-and-go penalty for speeding.

Any of the following violations will get you a black flag: exceeding the pit road speed limit, passing a car under the caution, and passing the pace car.

"I CAN'T DRIVE 55"

And you thought driving 55 mph on the interstate was tough! It's quite a transition. After touring Talladega at 200 mph, you then have to slow to a crawl on the pit road.

The NASCAR officials aren't kidding about the speed limit. It's 55 mph on the pit road, and that means that 56 mph is a violation. Play it safe and keep your speed to about 53 or 54 mph. You might lose a position to another car, but that's better than being called to the pits under the green.

The start of the pit road—at least as far as the speed limit is concerned—is marked by the beginning of the pit wall between the track and the pit lane. Make sure you've slowed to 55 mph by the time you reach this point. At the other end of the pits, you can accelerate past 55 mph once you've passed the end of the pit wall. You can also mark the end of the pits with the pace car. When you pass the pace car, feel free to hit the gas.

Figure 4.8
"Heck, I don't need that fender on a short track." Don't worry about fixing it.

TIP

If you're getting burned by the pit-road speed limit, toggle on the Braking Help option with the ALT-B command as you prepare to enter the pits. When you leave your pits, Braking Help will keep your speed at the required 55 mph, and then let you accelerate when you pass the white stripe. Be careful, though, even with Braking Help on. If you keep the gas pedal to the floor, your speed will sometimes creep to 56 mph, and you'll get penalized. Braking Help has no effect at Talladega.

CAR DAMAGE

When you bang into something, you usually damage the car. There are various degrees of damage, and the severity of the wreckage dictates how you should respond. Sometimes you have no choice but to pit immediately. In other cases, you can ignore a few dents until you have time to fix them.

SHORT TRACKS

Crumpled fenders and banged-up bumpers are as much a part of short-track racing as fried chicken and guys with beer guts. Don't worry too much about slight damage on a short track. A dent or two won't slow you down at all, and you'll lose valuable time in the pits while your crew makes some cosmetic repairs.

Later, if you have a lap on the field, you might tell the crew to fix the damage, but it really isn't necessary. On the half-mile tracks, racers wear a little body damage like medals of valor.

Remember to order your pit crew not to repair damage. Hit F9 to see the pit board. If it says "Repair Damage," hit the Enter key to toggle that command to "Do Not Repair Damage."

WHEN AERODYNAMICS COUNT

The slight body damage you ignore on the short tracks can be a serious problem on the bigger, faster tracks. When you're racing at 140 mph or faster, the car's aerodynamics become a critical factor. A crumpled fender can cost you 5 mph to 10 mph, or more, depending on the severity of the damage.

If your little wreck didn't bring out a caution flag, you're faced with a big decision. At the medium-length tracks—where top speed isn't the critical factor—you may choose to stay on the track and hope for a quick yellow flag so that you can pit under caution. You'll lose ground, but you might be able to stay in the lead lap if you catch a caution. If you don't get a yellow flag, however, you'll have to pit under green, and you'll have lost time on the track running at reduced speed.

At Talladega—and perhaps at Michigan, too—staying on the track with body damage is a more risky gamble. Depending on the extent of the damage, your straightaway speed will be drastically reduced. If you're unlucky enough not to draw a yellow flag, you should probably pit right away.

Since you have to stop anyway, go ahead and take on fuel and tires. You might be able to extend the next green-flag run, catch a caution at an opportune moment, and get back on the lead lap.

COMPUTER CARS AND THE PITS

The rules governing pit strategy for the computer-controlled cars are much the same as your own thinking. Like you, computer-controlled cars watch the leader and tend to follow his lead, pitting when he does and staying out when he stays out.

Of course, they also monitor fuel consumption and tire wear, though they're a bit conservative. They won't run their fuel down to the last gallon, or wear their tires down to the hub, like you can.

The computer drivers have a pretty sound pit strategy, but they lack the conniving guile of players like yourself. They're not able to look ahead and stop out of sequence to get just enough fuel to go to the finish. They run until they're low on fuel or tires, and then they pit.

RUNNING FOR THE TITLE

The Series Championship

WHY **SHOULD YOU CARE ABOUT THE CHAMPIONSHIP? BECAUSE** it's a big deal, that's why. NASCAR rewards its champions handsomely, and these are the racers that folks remember when they talk about the all-time greats: Petty, Earnhardt, Waltrip.

It's a grueling test of driving skill: about more races on a demanding variety of tracks, from tiny Martinsville to mighty Talladega, from the twisting turns of Sears Point to the lightning-fast high banks of Bristol. If you can win the championship in this game—with opponents at 100% and without cheating—you just might be ready for the real thing.

THE POINTS SYSTEM

The Winston Cup points system that determines the overall champion has been a subject of debate for years. The system rewards consistency above all else, so much so that critics say it doesn't place enough emphasis on winning. For example, if the second-place finisher led more laps than the winner, the second-place guy gets the same number of points, 180.

It may not be perfect, but the Winston Cup system consistently produces hotly contested races. And few could argue about the greatness of the drivers who have claimed the title since the first championship was awarded in 1949.

CONSISTENCY COUNTS

The race winner usually gets the most points, but over the course of a 30-race season, an also-ran who consistently finishes in the top 10 will fare better in the points standings than an erratic winner. With only 72 points separating first place from 20th in the points allocation, the top priority becomes finishing the race.

Figure 5.1
Winning races isn't enough to claim the crown of series champion.

Just ask Rusty Wallace. In 1994, Wallace led all drivers with six wins, but lost out in the title chase to Dale Earnhardt, who scored three wins on the season. A string of wrecks and poor finishes cost Wallace the championship, while Earnhardt finished in the top five nearly every week. That consistency paid off with a seventh title for the "Intimidator."

GETTING THE POINTS

HOW IT WORKS
The Winston Cup points system awards 175 points to the race winner, with a five-point drop-off for each position through the top 6. Positions 7 through 11 are seperated by four points; and 12 through 40 are seperated by three points. In addition, any driver who leads a lap gets five bonus points, and another five points goes to the the driver who leads the most laps, for a total of 185 possible points going to the winner.

The Winston Cup Points System

1	175	11	130	21	100	31	70
2	170	12	127	22	97	32	67
3	165	13	124	23	94	33	64
4	160	14	121	24	91	34	61
5	155	15	118	25	88	35	58
6	150	16	115	26	85	36	55
7	146	17	112	27	82	37	52
8	142	18	109	28	79	38	49
9	138	19	106	29	76	39	46
10	134	20	103	30	73	40	43

ODD DRIVERS OUT

The computer-controlled cars that are entered in the events in the order in which they appear in the Opponents section of the Driver Info menu. That sequence also appear in the "driver2.txt" file in the C:\NASCAR\CARS subdirectory containing that car set. And that's also how they line up on the pit road. Your car is first, followed by the #50 car, then Rusty Wallace in the #2, and so on.

The last few cars won't be included in the smaller fields that run on the short tracks. At Richmond, for example, the starting field is made up of 28 cars. That means that the last 11 computer cars won't even start the race, and they'll get no points.

To change who gets left out, use the Paint Kit to swap car graphics, bringing someone up from the end of the list to one of the positions that is guaranteed a starting spot, swapping that car for one you'd rather leave out. Don't forget to switch the entries for those drivers in the "driver2.txt" file, so that the names will match the new car graphics.

BENEFITTING FROM THE MISFORTUNE OF OTHERS

Since you own the game, you get to compete in every race, no matter how dismal your qualifying effort. Those poor guys on the last few rungs of the ladder have to sit out the short-track races, getting zero points for their effort. You, on the other

Figure 5.2
Side-by-side racing can lead to quick disaster. If you're in the hunt for the points championship, maybe you should let #30 get by.

hand, always make the field. That's significant, since 28th—dead last at Richmond—gives you 79 points at Richmond.

CHAMPIONSHIP STRATEGY

I admit it. It takes great patience and an unhealthy dedication to this game to make a real championship run. You have to be willing to drive a wrecked car that's running 20 mph slower than the rest of the field, or to patch up your battered race car and then get back on the track five laps down to run 300 more laps at the grueling Dover Downs.

But if you don't take it that seriously, you're not gonna win the championship. You can cheat, of course, saving and replaying races until you get it right. Yes, you can ensure that you'll win the title every year. But what would Junior Johnson have to say about that? Why, he'd probably give you the back of his big hand.

The strategy to winning a championship is simple, yet it's hard to accomplish. All you have to do is win on the tracks where you're really fast, place in the top-5 or top-10 on the tracks where you're pretty fast, and aim for a top-20 finish on the tracks where you really stink up the place.

NASCAR Winston Cup Champions

Year	Champion	Year	Champion
1994	Dale Earnhardt	1971	Richard Petty
1993	Dale Earnhardt	1970	Bobby Isaac
1992	Alan Kulwicki	1969	David Pearson
1991	Dale Earnhardt	1968	David Pearson
1990	Dale Earnhardt	1967	Richard Petty
1989	Rusty Wallace	1966	David Pearson
1988	Bill Elliott	1965	Ned Jarrett
1987	Dale Earnhardt	1964	Richard Petty
1986	Dale Earnhardt	1963	Joe Weatherly
1985	Darrell Waltrip	1962	Joe Weatherly
1984	Terry Labonte	1961	Ned Jarrett
1983	Bobby Allison	1960	Rex White
1982	Darrell Waltrip	1959	Lee Petty
1981	Darrell Waltrip	1958	Lee Petty
1980	Dale Earnhardt	1957	Buck Baker
1979	Richard Petty	1956	Buck Baker
1978	Cale Yarborough	1955	Tim Flock
1977	Cale Yarborough	1954	Lee Petty
1976	Cale Yarborough	1953	Herb Thomas
1975	Richard Petty	1952	Tim Flock
1974	Richard Petty	1951	Herb Thomas
1973	Benny Parsons	1950	Bill Rexford
1972	Richard Petty	1949	Red Byron

WIN WHERE YOU CAN WIN

Every driver has his or her favorite tracks, places where they've won before and are confident they can win again. Even as your skills improve and you can run up front on any track, you'll still have your favorites. Mine are: Talladega, Bristol, Martinsville, Michigan, Charlotte, and Atlanta. I've won on other tracks, but I *know* I should win races at these tracks. When I don't, I feel I've lost ground in the points race.

Figure 5.3
Take it easy at the start of a race. Avoiding the early wrecks will help ensure that you're still around for the checkered flag.

Any driver with a bit of experience should have two automatic victories every season: Talladega. Unless you crash or get burned on your pit-stop strategy, you should win every time out on this superspeedway.

The other tracks aren't nearly as easy, but you'll identify the tracks that suit your style. On these tracks, focus on not screwing up. If you know you have a car fast enough to win the race, there's no point in pushing the car too hard in the first few laps. Take it easy, conserve your equipment, and stay off the wall. If your car feels unstable running side-by-side with other cars early in the race, then let them pass. The real race, the NASCAR boys like to say, doesn't begin until the last 100 miles.

ENDURE THE TOUGHEST TRACKS

Then there are the tracks that just don't like you. While the other cars roar around the track as if they're on rails, you slip and slide all over the place, trying to survive lap by lap. Naturally, I don't feel that way about *any* tracks. But if I did, they would be Sears Point, Watkins Glen, Phoenix, and New Hampshire.

If your bad tracks are really bad, you should concentrate just on finishing the race. Who knows, if enough cars crash—

Figure 5.4
Atlanta is one
of the easier
tracks. You should
count on a top-10
finish here.

through no fault of yours, of course—you might be able to salvage a top-20 finish.

Think of these races as practice. It may not be fun to run for two or three hours on a track that you'd like to see turned into a parking lot, but you'll be a better driver for it. You'll be a little faster each time you visit these hated tracks, and someday you'll surprise yourself by running up front.

MAKING THE BEST OF A BAD RACE

Even at your best tracks, a few races just don't work out. You may get caught up in a wreck, or nod off and hit the wall, or screw up on a pit stop. Whatever the reason, you find yourself down a lap or more in a championship points race. What should you do? Why, tough it out, of course!

It's obvious but it's worth noting: when you quit a race, you'll finish behind every other car that's still running. But if you stay on the track and finish—even without the faintest chance of winning the race—you'll finish ahead of every driver that drops out.

If you're just a lap or two down—and you have a fast car— you should race hard to get those laps back. A timely caution flag might put you right back in contention for the win. When you're many laps down, with a damaged car, you should just

Figure 5.5
If you're weak on the road courses, then map out a strategy to survive and finish as high in the standings as possible.

try to stay out of the way of the faster cars. Try to finish, but there's no need to race against cars that are several laps ahead.

SMART PIT STOPS

A careful pit strategy can win races for you, and it can also salvage a decent finish out of a disastrous race. Pit under the yellow flag at every opportunity. Every time the caution flag flies, duck into the pits for fuel and tires, even if you were in the pits just a few laps before.

That extra gas and fresher tires will give you an edge over the rest of the field. It may be a slight edge, just a few laps worth of extra fuel. Or it may be a significant advantage, allowing you to run 20 or 30 laps farther on a green-flag run.

After you pit out of sequence with everybody else, cross your fingers and hope for a long run of green-flag racing. If you get lucky and don't get a caution, the other cars may be forced to pit under green, and you'll make up a lot of ground. Now it's time to pray for a caution, so that you can pit under yellow and hold onto the advantage you gained.

DRIVING A WRECK

Wrecks are pretty common in *NASCAR Racing*, and it seems you're involved in most of them. You *will* wreck, sometimes

Figure 5.6
Car #33 is turning
up the pressure.
Even with a dam-
aged car, you
might be able to
hold him off it
you stay in the
racing groove.

early in the race. And rarely is the damage terminal. You can usually limp back to the pits, make repairs, and rejoin the race—maybe laps down and the slowest car on the track. But if you stick to it, and play some smart pit strategy, you can still wind up with a decent finish, plus the points that go with it.

Of course, if nobody falls out of the race, you still might finish dead last. You'll spend all that time, having very little fun, driving a wrecked race car for no points' gain at all. So look on the bright side. At least you didn't spend those three hours strapped into a tiny seat, wearing a helmet, fire-proof suit, and gloves in the 120-degree heat. At least I *hope* you didn't.

IF YOU MUST CHEAT . . .

Like other aspects of *NASCAR Racing*, there are various ways to cheat to gain an advantage in the season points race. And like the others, I'll argue against cheating. This game is too good for cheating, and it's pretty easy to outwit your thick-headed computer opponents. But if you must cheat . . .

CHANGING HISTORY

The ability to save and restart races is like a powerful, built-in cheating tool. That's why Papyrus didn't include that option in the first version of *IndyCar Racing*. These guys go for realism, and stopping in the middle of a race to grab a bite to eat just

Figure 5.7
Sometimes you just get unlucky. Hold on tight and hope the damage isn't too severe.

isn't realistic. But it's only a game, after all, so they gave NASCAR players the ability to save a race.

That ability also gives you the power to change the course of history, or at least the course of a race. By saving the race at regular intervals—during each caution flag, for example—you can always return to that point if you crash and burn on the next restart.

TIP

Even if you don't plan to cheat, it's a good idea to save a race during caution periods. That way a power failure won't cost you two or three hours of hard-fought racing. But when you save during a caution, wait until you get the "One Lap Until Green" message. If you don't, any cars that are on the pit road when you exit will have to pit again—under green—when you restart the race. Now that's *cheating!*

SLOW DOWN THE OTHER GUYS

They say cheaters never win, but of course they sometimes do, especially in computer games. If you're getting blown away on a couple of tracks—and you just can't stand it—then reduce the opponents' strength in the Game Options menu. Let's not call this cheating; instead, let's think of it as an effort to create parity. NASCAR likes its racing close, and it isn't really competitive if you can't keep up, is it?

Use this trick as a last alternative, and try to keep increasing the opponent strength on a particular track as you get faster. And don't go wild with the adjustment. If you're getting outrun by only 1 or 2 mph, don't knock down opponent strength by 10%. Race with opponents at 97% or 98%, slowing them just enough to let you race with the slower cars in the field.

THE SCHEDULE

Assuming you have the *Track Pack* from Papyrus, the season schedule is made up of 28 races. If you don't have the *Track Pack*, mark the page and put this book down, go to the store, and get it . . . There, that's better. Now you're really ready to make a championship run.

During the season, you'll run two races at each of 12 tracks, and make a single visit to Sears Point, Watkins Glen, New Hampshire, and Phoenix. Consider that a stroke of good luck, since those are the toughest tracks for most players to master.

Season Schedule

February 27	Rockingham	500 miles
March 6	Richmond	400 laps
March 13	Atlanta	500 miles
March 27	Darlington	500 miles
April 10	Bristol	500 laps
April 17	North Wilkesboro	400 laps
April 24	Martinsville	500 laps
May 1	Talladega	500 laps
May 15	Sears Point	90 laps
May 29 (night)	Charlotte	600 miles
June 5	Dover Downs	500 miles

June 12	Pocono	500 miles
June 19	Michigan	400 miles
July 10	Loudon	300 laps
July 17	Pocono	500 miles
July 24	Talladega	500 miles
August 14	Watkins Glen	90 laps
August 21	Michigan	400 miles
August 27 (night)	Bristol	500 laps
September 4	Darlington	500 miles
September 10 (night)	Richmond	400 laps
September 18	Dover Downs	500 miles
September 25	Martinsville	500 laps
October 2	North Wilkesboro	400 laps
October 9	Charlotte	500 miles
October 23	Rockingham	500 miles
October 30	Phoenix	400 kilometers
November 13	Atlanta	500 miles

PRACTICE, PRACTICE

You won't always have enough time to run a race, or even time enough to run more than a few laps. If you'd still like to turn a few laps, go to Preseason Practice and visit one of your least-favorite tracks. Every lap helps you gain experience and a better understanding of the line, so you might see some improvement when that track comes up on the schedule.

MODIFYING THE SEASON

You don't have to include all the tracks on your season schedule. By editing the season file, you can set up the season's events any way you like. This makes you commissioner of the sanctioning body, in addition to your roles of driver, car owner, and chief mechanic.

So if you just can't compete on the road courses, drop 'em from the schedule. I know you're tormented by the possibility that this might be cheating, but don't fret too much. There are

Figure 5.8
There you are, hoisting the trophy in the winner's circle. (Who are all those people, anyway?)

plenty of real drivers who'd jump at the chance to drop their worst track from the schedule.

Here's how to do it. Find the file named "calendar" in the main game directory, C:\NASCAR. With a text editor, such as Windows' NotePad, open the file and delete the hated track. Most of the tracks host two events during the season, so make sure to delete both.

You can also change the order of the events. For example, since the 2.5-mile Daytona Speedway isn't included in the game (because of licensing reasons), I changed the schedule to open with a race at Talladega, letting that track take the place of the Daytona 500.

Using Talladega to represent the missing Daytona track leaves me with four events every season at Talladega. Since I win every time out at Talladega, that might seem a bit unfair. Heck, it's just one of them racin' deals.

RUNNING MORE THAN ONE SEASON
You can also run multiple seasons at the same time by working with two files, the "calendar" file and the "season.bin" file, which is also located in the main directory, C:\NASCAR.

In Chapter 7, I'll show you how to set up various racing series, such as the Busch Grand National, the International Race of Champions, and even an old-time NASCAR-greats series. There are good car-sets available for all of those series, but more on that in Chapter 7. For now, let's look at how to manipulate the files to let you run more than one season at a time.

You'll need to save versions of those two files under different names, one for each season you're running. For example, let's say you want to run two seasons, a regular Winston Cup series and a full season with old-timers like Junior Johnston and Fireball Roberts.

After you finish your first Winston Cup race, go to a file manager program like Window's File Manager. Go to the main NASCAR directory, C:\NASCAR. Find the "calendar" file (it has no extension), and rename it "calendar.wc." Then locate the "season.bin" file and rename it "season.wc."

Now start *NASCAR Racing*. Assuming you're using two different car sets, go to Player Info on the main menu and switch to the old-timers car set. Start a new Championship Season, run the race, and then exit from the game and find those two files. The two new "calendar" and "season.bin" files are for your old-timers series. Rename those files to "calendar.old" and "season.old." Now give the Winston Cup files their original names, "calendar" and "season.bin," and you're ready to run a race in the other series.

THE TRACKS

Taming the Tracks

NO **RACING SERIES IN THE WORLD RUNS SUCH A DIZZYING VARIETY** of race tracks. One week you're hurtling around Talladega at 200 mph, and the next week you're muscling your way through the tight turns at Martinsville at 65 mph. You'll have to get to know each of these tracks intimately in order to win, especially if you expect to capture the series title. Here's a description of each heading in the track sections.

TRACK STATISTICS

This is the basic data on the racetrack, including the length, banking at turns, all-time winningest driver, and the one-lap record. Pay attention to the degree of banking; it will give you a clue how fast you can drive through those corners, and what line to take. Included in the Track Statistics section is fuel consumption. Fuel mileage varies wildly, depending on gearing, your driving style, and where you are on the track. These estimates are meant to be a general measure of fuel mileage. You should check the Fuel display (F3) every now and then to see if your mileage falls within these ranges. You may come up short, or you may be able to stretch mileage a little further.

Mileage on the road courses varies even more than on the ovals, so watch fuel consumption carefully, and be ready to change your strategy if you aren't getting the mileage you expected. If you gamble and lose on mileage on a long, flat road course, you're probably done for the day.

RACE LENGTH OPTIONS

I like numbers to be nice and round, so I've listed race lengths in 100-mile segments, whenever it makes sense. Sometimes it isn't that neat, but I've applied those same percentages—100%,

80%, 60%, 50%, and 40%—to the races that aren't measured in miles.

Also included here are the estimated number of pits stop required if the race runs green. Remember, these are just estimates to help you plan strategy; you should carefully monitor your own fuel consumption.

A question mark after the pit-stop number means that making it to the finish on that number of stops isn't a sure thing. Check your mileage during a long practice session or the first green-flag run during the race before you decide to gamble.

SET-UP

Here you'll find a general discussion of chassis set-up and gearing for the track, along with a list of the set-ups that are included on the disc. A much more detailed discussion of car set-up is in Chapter 2. If you want to start from scratch, refer to that section.

THE GROOVE

The track graphic is the best way to visualize the fast line, but this section includes a description of braking and acceleration techniques required for each race track. The line inside the track represents the racing groove. Remember, though, that some tracks have more than one groove, so yours might differ slightly from the one shown.

The numbers on the graphic show the fastest possible (I think) speeds at various points around the track: at the start/finish line, entering the turns, mid-way through the turns, and exiting the turns.

The average speed, along with the interval speeds, is for a *very fast* lap, run with a race set-up. You should think of these speeds as goals. At Rockingham, for example, don't think that you have to be going 130 mph in the middle of the corners to turn a good lap. But if you're hitting 120 mph at that spot, you know you can get through that turn just a little faster.

If you can reach the average lap speeds shown in the graphic, you'll blow the doors off the rest of the field every time out. Don't worry about matching those speeds. If you can *approach* those lap speeds—usually within 3 or 4 mph—you'll outrun computer opponents set at 100% strength.

PASSING

Here you'll find the best places to pass on each track. Sometimes your passing opportunities are limited to one or two. On other tracks there are several passing lanes. Of course, don't feel restricted to those shown here. These will work, but sometimes you can establish new passing lanes based on your individual driving style.

PIT STRATEGY

This section includes an overview of pit strategy, factoring in the typical tire wear you might experience at the track. You'll find out whether it's usually smart to stay out during cautions and gain track position, or whether you should probably pit at every opportunity.

North Carolina Motor Speedway

This one-mile tri-oval in the sand hills of North Carolina is the site of some of the longest and most grueling races on the Winston Cup circuit. Tight and fast, "The Rock" isn't a favorite of many drivers. It's pretty much a one-groove race track, so if you miss the set-up or can't find the line consistently, you're in for a very long day.

Figure 6.1
The treacherous fourth-turn exit claims another victim at The Rock.

Track Statistics

Length	1.017 miles
Banking, Turns 1 & 2	22 degrees
Banking, Turns 3 & 4	25 degrees
Lap record	156.099 (Ricky Rudd)
Full fuel run	100–110 laps

Race Length Options

100%	500 miles	492 laps	4 stops
80%	400 miles	394 laps	3 stops
60%	300 miles	296 laps	2 stops
50%	250 miles	246 laps	2 stops
40%	200 miles	197 laps	1 stop

SET-UP

The stock Ace set-up is fast enough to win at 100% opponent strength, but you can still tweak the set-up to better suit your driving style.

Cornering is the key here, so you'll want the maximum angle on the rear spoiler to provide downforce.

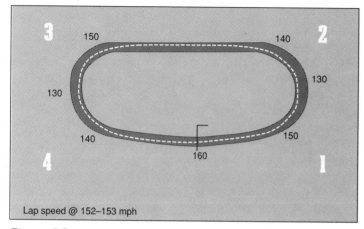

Figure 6.2

A loose car will make for a long day at The Rock, so try to build a little push into the chassis. Try setting the right-side shocks a bit stiffer than those on the left side. For smaller adjustments, try increasing the cross-weight slightly.

THE GROOVE

Enter turn 1 about one lane above the bottom of the track, sweeping down as low on the banking as you can and still hold the car through turns 1 and 2. Let the car drift up the track as you exit turn 2, and then ride along the outside wall down the backstretch. The line through turns 3 and 4 is the same, except that you have to deal with the dogleg down the frontstretch. The car wants to break loose here, so be ready to straighten it out as you approach the start/finish line.

In 1965, the legendary Curtis Turner drove the Woods Brothers Ford to victory in the American 500, the inaugural race at the North Carolina Motor Speedway. For Turner, known as a hard-driving man—on and off the track—it was his first NASCAR win since 1956. Four years earlier, NASCAR had banned Turner for attempting to organize a drivers' union.
• Turner was a fan favorite, but his rough style ruffled the feathers of some drivers. At a dirt track in Charlotte, Turner was unable to pass

leader Tiny Lund, so he shoved Lund off the track, over the guardrail, and into the parking lot. Afterward, Tiny—all 6'8" and 280 pounds of him—grabbed Turner and started dunking him in a lake. Fearing for his life, Turner promised to buy Lund a new car.

A gentle touch on the brake pedal is one of the keys to turning fast laps at The Rock. Don't charge into the turns at full throttle. Instead, lift off the gas earlier than you think you have to, and then brake lightly to get your speed down to about 150 mph or slower as you begin turning into the corner. Feather the throttle (if you're using pedals) or repeatedly tap the throttle key to keep your speed near 130 mph through the corner.

PASSING

In the game, at least, Rockingham is a one-groove race track, so passing is extremely difficult. A typical race finds cars running in tight, single-file packs. You'll probably have to work your way through the field one car at a time.

Exit speed coming off the turns is critical to passing at The Rock. You'll have to get beside the lead car quickly to pull off a pass before you get to the next corner. Look to pass coming out of turn 4. If you can maintain traction here, you can dive to the inside of the leading car through the dogleg at the start/finish line. If you have enough straightaway speed, move to the inside down the backstretch, and then outbrake the other car going into the turns. This is a tough pass, since the fast line entering the turns is about a car-width up the track.

There is a pretty fast high groove here, but it takes some nerve to run it. When you can't get inside of another car, try driving into turn 1 a little deeper, letting the car drift to the outside of the lead car. If you can get back on the gas soon enough—and keep the car off the wall—you can sometimes pull off the pass down the backstretch.

PIT STRATEGY

Even if you can't manage to pass cars under green, you can win races at Rockingham by stretching your green-flag runs. Tire wear shouldn't be a factor; the tires ought to last a full fuel run. Keep that in mind when you decide whether or not to pit under caution. If you're far back in the pack, with a half-tank of gas, consider staying out if a yellow flag flies. You might gain a dozen positions, and with passing so tough, the other drivers will have a hard time getting back around you.

Richmond

This ¾-mile, D-shaped track is one of the trickiest ovals on the circuit. Rebuilt in 1988 to replace the old ½-mile Richmond Fairgrounds Raceway, the new facility is smooth and wide. It looks inviting enough, but the racing groove is narrow, flat, and treacherous. Richmond is the site of one of the circuit's three night races.

Track Statistics

Length	.759 miles
Banking	14 degrees
Lap record	124.052 (Ted Musgrave)
Full fuel run	150 laps

Race Length Options

100%	300 miles	400 laps	2 stops
80%	243 miles	320 laps	2 stops
60%	182 miles	240 laps	1 stop
50%	152 miles	200 laps	1 stop
40%	121 miles	160 laps	no stops

SET-UP

The quick set-ups for Richmond work for a blend of short-track handling and superspeedway drafting on the straightaways.

Figure 6.3
Two cars battle for position as they head out of turn 4 and toward the dogleg.

Starting with the Ace set-up, try to loosen up the car just a bit, so that the back end wants to swing out through the turns. It'll be tough to drive on cold tires, but you'll be faster after the right-front tire heats up and the car begins to develop a push. Experiment with softer springs to let the car move high or low on the track to pass. Knock the rear spoiler up to the maximum height allowed.

There is no one ultimate set-up for Richmond. More than any other track, set-up here is largely a matter of individual driving style. Start with the Ace settings, and then work with shocks, tire pressures, and weights to find a combination that helps you turn your quickest, most consistent laps.

THE GROOVE

The key to quick laps here is the dogleg down the front straightaway. If you can hit the right line through the dogleg, you'll carry more speed into turn 1 and more speed down the backstretch. This takes plenty of nerve and a sure-footed chassis, because you have to run right up against the wall to maintain traction and be able to accelerate through the start/finish line. A slightly loose set-up will help, but you have to be good enough to keep the car's rear end from slapping the concrete.

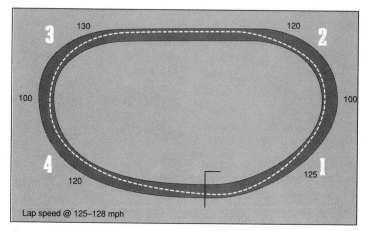

Figure 6.4

The line through the corners is pretty much the same: Enter turns 1 and 3 about a lane up from the bottom of the track, and then keep the car as low as possible through the middle of the corner. Drift up to the outside wall down the straightaway, and then move low as you enter the turn.

To accelerate quickly coming off turn 4, you have to aim the car just to the right of the end of pit wall. It takes a bit of nerve to keep the car that low. A slight miscalculation will send you head-on into the concrete. But if you swing too far above that low groove, you won't be able to get on the gas fast enough as you exit the turn.

Cornering at Richmond is a lot like walking on egg shells. It takes finesse to tip-toe through the wide, flat turns. The faster set-ups are a bit loose and twitchy, so be prepared for a full day's work running a race here.

You'll use plenty of brakes going into the turns. Get the car slowed quickly enough so that you're at the bottom of the track before you reach the middle of the turn. If you're not low, you won't be able get back on the gas soon enough or hard enough to get the straightaway speed you need.

PASSING

Richmond is a tighter race track than it first appears, so you can't pass with abandon just anywhere on the track. If you can stick to the bottom of the track through the turns, you can pass short-track style, moving under the lead car when it slips up the track. But if you try to dive to the inside before you reach the corner, you won't be able to drive as deep into the turn as the car on the outside. The best bet for passing in the turns is to ride the lead car's bumper, and then take advantage of a mistake or try to out-accelerate him coming out of the corner.

The dogleg is probably your best chance at passing a fast car. Stay as close as you can to the car in front—even if you have to give the other a guy a little nudge—and then follow him up to the outside wall coming out of turn 4. As you cross the start/finish line, dive to the left and get inside position before you enter turn 1.

PIT STRATEGY

Your pit strategy here is determined mainly by how much wear you can squeeze out of your tires. If you can run smooth, consistent laps without abusing the right-front tire, then you can make the rubber last a full fuel run. When you don't have to worry about tire wear, you can run a 300-mile race at Richmond on just two pit stops. The trouble is, the fast groove around here is so elusive that it's hard to keep from sliding the right-front. And when you squeal that right-front tire lap after lap, it's not gonna last.

If you just can't seem to find the groove at Richmond (and you're not alone), then try to conserve tires and see if you can run the distance on one fewer pit stop than your competition. Consider pitting only when you're low on gas, even passing up stops during caution periods. You might be able to outsmart your faster competitors.

Atlanta

Measuring just over 1.5 miles, the oval track in Atlanta has emerged as one of the fastest circuits in NASCAR outside of the superspeedways at Talladega, Daytona, and Michigan. Cars hurtle around Atlanta at a breakneck pace. Slap the wall here, and you'll probably need a new race car.

Track Statistics

Length	1.522 miles
Banking	24 degrees
Lap record	185.830 (Greg Sacks)
Full fuel run	60–65 laps

Race Length Options

100%	500 miles	328 laps	4 stops
80%	400 miles	263 laps	3 stops?
60%	300 miles	197 laps	2 stops?
50%	250 miles	164 laps	2 stops
40%	200 miles	131 laps	1 stop?

SET-UP

Despite its speed, Atlanta is primarily a handling race track. You'll want plenty of rear spoiler to provide enough downforce to increase cornering speed, but that's a trade-off of top speed on the straightaways. Start with the rear spoiler set to maximum, and then experiment with a little less to see how little you can get by with and still feel comfortable negotiating the corners.

A loose race car can be a real bear to handle in the high-speed corners of Atlanta, so try to set up the car a little tight. Be careful, though, because cars tend to develop a push anyway

Figure 6.5
The draft is very effective down the high-speed straightaways of Atlanta.

during long green-flag runs. If you start out too tight, you may not be able to keep the car off the wall after 20 or 30 laps.

During the race, be ready to made a slight wedge adjustment to help ease understeer. If the car's too loose to handle, try adding a pound or two of cross-weight. As always, be careful with mid-race adjustments. Go too far in one direction and you might feel like you're driving a tractor.

THE GROOVE

Atlanta is one of the few symmetrical race tracks on the circuit. It's a true oval, so the lines through the corners are the same at each end of the speedway.

Hug the outside wall down the straightaway, and then dive down the track as you enter the turn. You turn into the corners a little later and a little higher on the track than you've gotten used to at other tracks. If you're having trouble getting through the turns here, chances are you're starting to turn the wheel too soon. Try waiting a bit longer before turning left.

Atlanta is a fast race track, but having a lead foot isn't the secret to turning quick laps here. Driving into the corners too hard puts you out of shape for coming off the turn, and that cuts down on your straightaway speed headed into the next corner.

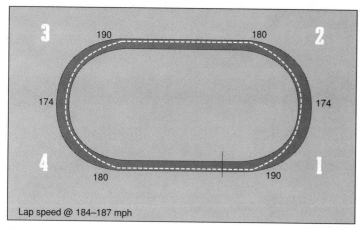

Lap speed @ 184–187 mph

Figure 6.6

While you turn into the corner a bit late here, you should get out of the gas a little earlier than you're accustomed to doing.

Try not to use the brakes. If you drive too deep into a turn, learn to tap the brakes just enough to get the car back down in the groove. The smoothest and fastest method, though, is to back off on the gas just a touch sooner.

PASSING

The track is wide, it's smooth, and it invites lots of passing, at several points on the speedway. If you've got the horsepower, there's enough straightaway here to complete a pass and clear the other car before you reach the turn. The key here is "getting a good run off the corner," running a good enough line through the corner to keep traction as you accelerate out of the turn. If you're close to the lead car and gaining as you come off the turn, you can pull past the lead car and get back into line before you reach the next corner. The draft is very much in play at Atlanta, though it's not the dominant factor that it is at Talladega.

You can also pull off a pass in the turns, but if the lead car is almost equal to yours, it can get dicey as you work the bottom of the track. The car tends to "bind up" because it's making a sharper turn than the car on the outside. You lose RPMs, making it tough to out-accelerate the other car off the turn.

PIT STRATEGY

Passing is relatively easy at Atlanta, so a gamble on fuel mileage isn't as attractive as it is on other tracks. If you're fast, you can move through the pack pretty quickly. It's usually smart to trade a few positions for a new set of tires and a full tank of gas. Unless you just pitted, or you're feeling especially lucky, take advantage of caution flags. It's easy to burn up the right-front tire, too, so you'll probably welcome every chance you get to pit for new rubber.

Darlington

Darlington stands alone among race tracks, on the NASCAR circuit or anywhere else. The egg-shaped oval is arguably the most difficult track on the schedule, yet the drivers consider the races there to be among the most prestigious they run. It's narrow and bumpy, and you're fighting every lap to keep the car from slapping the wall. Many drivers consider Darlington's Southern 500 the most important race of the season; others think the place should be bulldozed.

Track Statistics	
Length	1.366 miles
Banking, turns 1 & 2	23 degrees
Banking, turns 3 & 4	25 degrees
Lap record	166.998 (Geoff Bodine)
Full fuel run	70–75 laps

Figure 6.7
The fast groove through the treacherous corners at Darlington is right up against the wall.

Race Length Options			
100%	500 miles	366 laps	4 stops
80%	400 miles	263 laps	3 stops
60%	300 miles	220 laps	2 stops
50%	250 miles	183 laps	2 stops
40%	200 miles	146 laps	1 stop?

SET-UP

You need the car to be a touch on the loose side, since you'll be struggling constantly to keep it off the wall on this tight track. Start with the Ace set-up, or one of the other Darlington set-ups, and start fine-tuning it to suit your driving style. You'll be running right against the wall anyway, so you want to be able to turn the car left smoothly and easily.

If the car tightens during the race, take a round of wedge out (decrease the cross-weight) during a pit stop. You'll want all the downforce you can muster, so bump the rear spoiler up to its highest setting.

THE GROOVE

Because the track was designed for much slower speeds, you have to use all the race track to get around Darlington well.

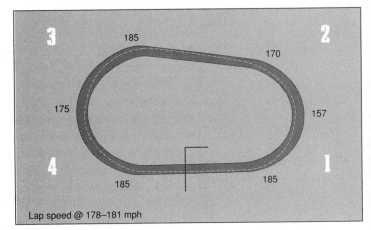

Figure 6.8

That means entering the turns higher than feels safe, diving to the bottom at the apex, and then letting your speed throw you right up against the outside wall as you head down the straightaway. It's a wild ride, and it takes some time to get a feel for it. Aside from the road courses, Darlington probably requires more practice time than any other track you'll run.

Enter turn 1 from the high groove, and then drive it right down to the bottom of the track before you reach the apex. Take the car out to the wall, and then prepare yourself for turns 3 and 4, maybe the toughest turns in all of stock-car racing. Enter turn 3 from the top of the track, and let it find the groove, which is right at the top of the track, almost brushing the wall. About half-way through turn 3, cut left and steer to the bottom lane as you reach the apex of turns 3 and 4. Climb gradually up the banking as you go through turn 4, and then drift out to the wall as you enter the straightaway (as if you have a choice!).

PASSING

Just driving around Darlington by yourself is challenging enough, but you'll probably be wanting to pass some other cars, since this is racin' and all. Actually, passing and running in traffic can be fun here, if you have a sure-footed car underneath you.

If you have a horsepower advantage (and you do), there's enough straightaway here to pull off a pass before you reach the next corner. Passing in the turns is a bit trickier. Since the fast groove is high on the track, that is often the best place to pass, especially in turns 3 and 4—if you have enough nerve to run even higher than the lead car.

Inside passes in the corners are a different matter. This works best in turns 1 and 2, where you enter the corner a little lower on the track anyway. If you drive into turn 3 on the inside of another car, though, there's gonna be trouble. Enter the turn at full speed and you're likely to slide up the banking and into the car on the outside. If you slow down enough to go low through the turn in good shape, the outside car will be able to out-accelerate you coming off the turn. If you can pull off an inside pass in turns 3 and 4, consider yourself an ace driver.

PIT STRATEGY

I got your pit strategy right here: enjoy your stops and relax for a few seconds before heading back out onto this treacherous track. Your tires should last for a full run on gas, so consider playing a fuel-mileage strategy, especially if you're getting outrun badly.

You're bound to smack the wall a few times during a race here, but you can usually wait for a caution to make repairs. Aerodynamics are a factor, but you usually won't lose more than a few miles an hour with a crumpled fender.

Bristol

Get ready for the ride of your life. They don't call Bristol the world's fastest ½-mile for nothing. Cars scream around this high-banked track at a dizzying pace—a 125 mph average or better. It's a flat-out thrilling track, even when there's not another car in sight. Put 30 other cars on the track, and a race here can turn into a demolition derby. Because the cars travel these high banks so fast, one-car wrecks are rare. A spinning car usually collects several others, leaving a track full of mangled metal.

WARNING ▬ ▬ ▬ ▬ ▬ ▬ ▬ ▬ ▬
Try not to pause a race at Bristol, except during cautions. This place is too fast, the track's too short, and it's too dangerous here to risk breaking your rhythm. If there's an dire emergency—let's say the pizza delivery guy is at the door—then try to pause the game as soon as you get the car straightened out coming off a turn.

▬ ▬ ▬ ▬ ▬ ▬ ▬ ▬ ▬ ▬ ▬ ▬ ▬

Track Statistics

Length	.533 miles
Banking	36 degrees
Lap record	124.946 (Chuck Bown)
Full fuel run	160–170 laps

Race Length Options

100%	266 miles	500 laps	2 stops?
80%	213 miles	400 laps	2 stops
60%	160 miles	300 laps	1 stop
50%	133 miles	250 laps	1 stop
40%	107 miles	200 laps	1 stop

SET-UP

You may want to use a tight set-up while you learn your way around Bristol, but you'll have to loosen it up to be really fast here. Start out with the Ace set-up. After you feel comfortable with it, adjust camber, tire pressures, and wedge for a looser, quicker set-up. The general rule is exaggerated at Bristol: the looser the set-up, the faster the car. Unfortunately, that also

Figure 6.9

A car spins out of control. On the high banks of Bristol, that usually means a bunch of mangled machinery.

results in a car that's more difficult to control, especially on cold tires.

Other set-up guidelines for short-track cars apply, as well: shorter gearing, maximum spoiler, and increased stagger. The 15-degree wheel lock in the Ace set-up can be deadly here. Reduce that to 10 degrees or less. You want just enough to steer the car high and low.

THE GROOVE

The fast line at Bristol is an exaggeration of the classic apex method of cornering. Enter the turns high and drive the car down to the lower-middle lane through the corners. Look for the groove about one lane up from the bottom of the track. Go through the turns too low and you won't be able to accelerate quickly enough off the turns.

Let the car climb the banking and straighten out near the wall as you head down the straightaways. The back end of the car wants to break loose coming out of the corners, especially as you exit turn 4. You'd better get comfortable keeping the back end behind you, especially on cold tires.

At least the track is symmetrical, though you can enter turn 1 slightly faster than turn 3. Depending on the gearing and how fast you're entering the turns, you should only have to tap the brakes as you enter the turns. As you top 140 mph at the end

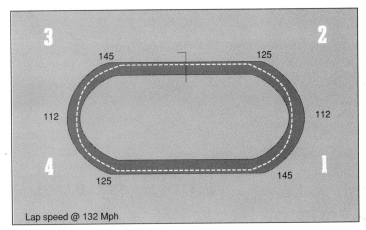

Figure 6.10

of the straights, gently tap the brakes to get the car to turn into the groove, and then immediately ease back into the throttle, feathering the gas until you can floor it coming off the turn.

PASSING

Running in heavy traffic is a harrowing experience at Bristol, but if you're turning quick times you can knock off two or three cars a lap. Be careful not to run over the cars in front of you, since they tend to get bunched up and slow down as they negotiate the turns.

Ride close behind the car in front and wait for a mistake. Sooner or later—and it's usually sooner—the lead car will get out of shape and slide up the banking and out of the groove. Just hold your line and you'll pass easily. Watch the mirror and pull in front of the other car as soon as you clear it, getting back-up into the fast groove as you head for the next corner.

PIT STRATEGY

Tire wear, especially on the rear tires, is your enemy at Bristol. There's so much tire spin coming off the corners that it's next to impossible to get your tires to last a full fuel run. With that in mind, you should take advantage of yellow flags to get tires and fuel. Long green-flag runs are rare here. The races are usually slowed by frequent caution periods.

Because of the high number of accidents and yellow flags, you might consider staying out during some of those yellow flags, especially if you're far back in the field. You can usually gain several positions on the race track, but you're gambling that there'll be another caution before you're forced to pit under green. If you're running in the top 5 or the top 10, watch the leaders and follow their lead. If you're in the lead, it's your call.

North Wilkesboro

Like all the NASCAR race tracks, North Wilkesboro is unique. When it was built in 1947 as a dirt track, the developer didn't have enough money to level the site, so the track was built on a hill. The front stretch runs downhill, while the back stretch climbs back up the hill. It's relatively flat, as NASCAR ovals go, with long, sweeping turns connected by two short chutes. This mountainous area of North Carolina once produced some of the finest moonshine in the country. Now the primary business here is fender-bending short-track racing at its best.

Track Statistics

Length	.625 miles
Banking	14 degrees
Lap record	119.016 (Ernie Irvan)
Full fuel run	140–145 laps

Race Length Options

100%	250 miles	400 laps	2 stops
80%	200 miles	320 laps	2 stops
60%	150 miles	240 laps	1 stop
50%	125 miles	200 laps	1 stop
40%	100 miles	160 laps	1 stop

Figure 6.11
Who says racing isn't a contact sport? This is business as usual in the heavy traffic at North Wilkesboro.

SET-UP

The low banking here demands a tighter set-up than you're probably used to running, but you'll be grateful for a little push in these relatively flat turns. Don't over-adjust on wedge or shock set-ups, though, because the car tends to push more here after a few laps. Try to start out fairly neutral, then you should get faster as the car develops a push after the tires heat up.

Starting with the Ace set-up, shorten the gearing by one or two steps all the way through the gearbox to give you greater acceleration off the corners. Watch out, though. If you're running a near-perfect line, you might over-rev at the ends of the straights.

PASSING

You'll earn every position you gain on this race track. It's basic stuff: chase 'em down and force 'em out of the inside groove through the corners. There's enough straightaway here to get alongside the lead car, but it's tough to clear the other car before you reach the next turn.

Don't be afraid to rub fenders at North Wilkesboro; sometimes that's what it takes. If that fellow in the black car just

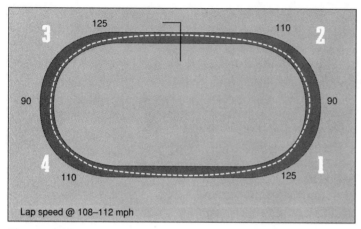

Lap speed @ 108–112 mph

Figure 6.12

won't give an inch of race track, remind him you're back there with a rap to the rear bumper. It might get his attention (OK, so it's just the computer driver), or it might knock him out of the groove.

With the right set-up—tight enough to punch the gas midway through the corner—you can pull of an outside pass here, but it's quite a trick. Remember, you probably have more room on the inside—between your car and the other guy's—than you think. Try to move further down on the other car to claim a lower, faster line. You'll know when you've gone too far. You'll hear the crunch of metal on metal.

PIT STRATEGY

Here's a track where you can use smart pit stops to pass cars that you can't get by on the track. Stretch your pit stops as far as you can under the green flag, and consider staying out during some caution periods if you have some tires and gas left.

As on the other short tracks, don't worry about body damage here, unless you just can't drive the car. "Cosmetic" damage won't slow the car much, and you'll lose a lap in the pits—even under the yellow flag—while your crew beats your car back into shape. Wait until you've got a lap on the field before you make repairs.

Martinsville

For the fans in attendance, this lovely speedway is like an oasis on the NASCAR circuit. For you, though, Martinsville means a couple of hours of intense, physical, fender-rubbing short-track action. "Frammin' and bammin,'" as Dale Earnhardt describes it.

Martinsville is the shortest and slowest track on the big-league NASCAR circuit, but that doesn't mean it's not exciting. In fact, there's nothing that quite matches the close-quarters racing thrills at Martinsville.

Track Statistics

Length	.526 miles
Banking	12 degrees
Lap record	94.185 (Ted Musgrave)
Full fuel run	150–155 laps

Race Length Options

100%	263 miles	500 laps	2 stops
80%	210 miles	400 laps	2 stops
60%	158 miles	300 laps	1 stop?
50%	132 miles	250 laps	1 stop
40%	105 miles	200 laps	1 stop

SET-UP

The game manual's on the mark here: use short, tight gearing for quick acceleration; and lean toward a loose set-up to give you more control so that you can get back on the gas in a hurry off the turns.

Assuming you aren't running a precisely perfect line on every lap, you can safely increase the fourth-gear ratio to 6.00,

Figure 6.13
The inside is the preferred line as you look to pass in Martinsville's tight turns.

one step above the Ace set-up gearing. You might also try increasing the stagger to make the car turn more easily.

THE GROOVE

The Martinsville is simple and brutal: get to the bottom of the track through the corners and hold that line. Drift out to the wall down the straightaways so that you can dive down to the bottom as you enter turns 2 and 3. Hold the inside line here and you can hold back Richard Petty himself.

You'll never run Martinsville really fast with Braking Help turned on. You can drive much deeper into the turns than the computer braking dude. Expect an extra 3 mph or more by doing the braking yourself.

TIP

Hit the brakes while the car is still traveling in a straight line, and then cut left. Slam on the brakes while your front wheels are turned left and you're likely to spin out.

Get on the brakes *hard* going into each corner. Luckily, Papyrus didn't model brake wear into the simulation, so you don't have to worry about losing your brakes, a common problem here

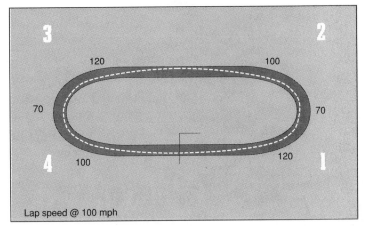

Figure 6.14

for real NASCAR drivers. You want to be doing about 70 mph, or slightly slower, at the slowest point in the middle of the turn. Don't brake until the car drops to that speed, or you'll be well below that speed by the time you get back on the gas. Instead, brake down to about 75 mph or so before you lift off the pedal (or key). The car will continue to slow until you get back on the gas.

PASSING

Traffic plays a critical role in passing at Martinsville. Although the straightaways aren't long enough to pull off a clean pass against a fast race car, the pack tends to bunch up and slow down in a chain reaction. If you can avoid the traffic jam and stay on the gas, you can pass two or three cars at a time.

Otherwise, passing is accomplished with the typical roughhouse short-track tactics. Get right on the lead car's bumper and put the pressure on through the turns. When you get a good run off the corner, you can pull alongside down the straightaway, and then finish the pass in the next corner. If you can't get alongside the lead car coming off the turns, just keep pressuring the lead car until the driver slips up the race track.

PIT STRATEGY

Keep a close watch on tire wear, especially that right front. Hard racing in traffic will burn it up in a hurry. When that happens, back off to cool the tire down, and then get back to a more conservative pace.

If you can save the right front, you can conceivably run a 500-lap race here on just two pit stops. If the race stays green and you pull this off, you will win the race.

Forget about cosmetic body damage. Bent fenders and tire marks on your doors are just part of short-track racing here. Race cars do not escape Martinsville unmarked.

Talladega

If you have an appetite for sheer speed, Talladega is your place. The longest closed speedway in the world, Talladega saw some of its drivers heading for 220 mph before NASCAR took steps to slow the speeds in the interest of safety. Even with mandated carburetor restrictor plates, reducing the flow of fuel to the engine, cars running in the draft can average 200 mph lapping this massive superspeedway.

Track Statistics

Length	2.66 miles
Banking, turns	33 degrees
Banking, tri-oval	18 degrees
Lap record	212.809 (Bill Elliott)
Full fuel run	48 laps

Race Length Options

100%	500 miles	188 laps	3 stops
80%	400 miles	150 laps	2 stops
60%	300 miles	113 laps	2 stops
50%	250 miles	94 laps	1 stop
40%	200 miles	75 laps	1 stop

Figure 6.15
The lead draft heads into turn 1 at over 190 mph, streaking away from the field.

SET-UP

When you're racing against computer-controlled cars, the Ace12 set-up is fast enough to outrun opponents with strength set as high as 102%. But if you're taking on the hot-shot driver across town or running in Papyrus's multi-player racing service, you'll need to squeeze a little more speed out of your Talladega set-up.

Try lowering the fourth-gear ratio by one or two steps. This will reduce your engine's RPMs at the end of the straightaways, but the car will still be accelerating as you enter the turns. Depending on your line, this may allow the car to maintain a faster speed through the turn. Play with the left and right bias settings, plus the wedge, to see if you can make the car match your driving style more comfortably. You probably won't gain any speed, but you might be able to make the car more stable in traffic.

THE GROOVE

The winning formula at Talladega is maybe 90% set-up and 10% driver. Your job behind the wheel is to keep the car pointed in the right direction and never lift off the gas.

TIP

Ready for a real thrill? You can remove the restrictor plate to unleash the full fury of 750 horsepower at Talladega. Use a text editor to open the "taladega.txt" file in the appropriate track subdirectory. Here's the path: C:\NASCAR\TRACKS\TALADEGA\TALADEGA.TXT. Find the line in this file that begins Spdwy. Change the first character after Spdwy from 1 to 0. When you go back out on the track, you're in for a surprise. Hold the gas pedal to the floor and you'll hit 220 mph or 230 mph by the time you reach the turn. Forget about holding it to the floor all the way around the track. You'll have to get off the gas, and maybe even tap the brakes to keep the car off the concrete. You'll be glad it's just a game. The computer cars aren't affected by this change, so you won't want to race like this, unless you really love to cheat.

As you already know if you've logged a few laps here, your only real challenge is the tri-oval, or dogleg, down the front stretch. Negotiating this section of the track is critical to turning a fast lap—not to mention keeping your car in one piece. The key is the approach. As you come off turn 4, take the car right up against the outside wall. Cut left across the track through the dogleg, right down almost to the grass. You'll come out of the dogleg close to the outside wall—you have no choice. If you cut left too late, you'll smack the wall hard. The black marks through the dogleg mark the line, but if you wait until you can see them it's too late. Hitting the line through here requires timing, and that will come only through practice. Look on the bright side. You only have to make it through the dogleg 188 times in a 500-mile race.

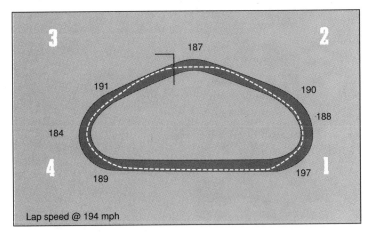

Figure 6.16

Learn to time the dogleg maneuver so that you have to turn the wheel or joystick as little as possible. Squealing the tires through here scrubs off speed and wears out the tires in a hurry.

The rest of the track is child's play: shoot down the backstretch on the outside, then go low through the corners. As you come off turn 4, try driving down low, putting the left-side tires below the white line. This will let you pick up 1 mph an hour, and every little bit helps here.

TIP

There's a bit of glitch in the programming for the computer cars at Talladega, and it should make you the driver to beat every time out. The computer cars are programmed to be more aggressive in passing during braking. Since braking is not a factor at Talladega, they won't pull out to pass you. As long as you hold the preferred line, they won't be able to pass you, even if they're much faster. Just one slip, though, and they'll stream by you like a line of cars on a busy interstate.

PASSING

Of course, drafting is the key to passing at Talladega. As a car travels down the race track, it creates something of a vacuum behind it as it cuts through the air. A car riding behind the lead car meets less resistance from the air, so it gains 2 or 3 mph. The lead car also benefits from the draft, and picks up speed as well. The trailing car, though, picks up more speed and is sort of sucked up close to the lead car. All you have to do is let the draft pull you close to the rear bumper of the lead car, and then pull out and speed past. There's nothing the other guy can do.

TIP

The effects of the draft are especially damaging at the start of the race and on the restarts. As I discussed in Chapter 5, the player's car is slower than the computer-controlled cars on cold tires. That puts you at a serious disadvantage at Talladega, because that means you're going to lose the draft. It's maddening to watch the other cars slide by and pull away, but you have to be patient. The key is to qualify up front and not get blown away on the start. You should have no problem qualifying in the top-20, even with the opponents set to 100% strength or higher. When the green flag flies, get into line as quickly as you can. The cars in front of you are going to pull away, so keep as many cars behind you as possible.

The draft works its magic from several car-lengths back, so you don't have to be right on the lead car's bumper to feel the benefits. While the draft makes passing easy at Talladega, it makes for a long day when you fall behind. When you lose the draft, the cars in front will pull away. And there's very little you can do. Hopefully, you'll have a fast car right behind you to help you pick up speed. But as long as the cars in front stay in single file, you probably won't be able to catch them. Unless they fan out trying to pass one another—or until they catch slower traffic—you'll just have to wait for a caution to bunch up the field.

The racing at Talladega quickly settles into packs of cars, running a few or several seconds apart. You can quickly draft to the front of a pack; the tough part is catching the next group ahead. Use the draft to shoot past the pack. That may give you enough extra speed to close the gap on the next group. Hopefully, you can hook on to the draft of that pack and close on them, draft by, and go for the next group. Never, ever lift your foot off the gas, and turn the wheel as little as possible, while staying in the preferred line and negotiating the dogleg smoothly.

Once you catch the lead pack, you can easily shoot past to take the lead. Hold 'em off until you catch some slower cars, and then use your brilliant maneuvers in traffic to leave the rest of the field in the dust.

PIT STRATEGY

There aren't as many accidents at Talladega as on some other tracks, so races are often marked by long green-flag runs. That makes pit strategy critical, and you can use your pit "smarts" to win races. Your tires should last a full fuel stop, as long as you don't abuse them by erratic driving or by taking anything less than a smooth line through the tri-oval. Still, it's close. But you should be able to stretch tire wear until you need gas. You can often run the race on one fewer stop than the computer drivers. Many times, that alone will put you in winner's circle.

Bang up the car at Talladega, and you're in for a long day at the races. Aerodynamics mean speed here, and speed means everything. Sorry, Junior, but you'll have to bring it in. You have to fix it, but even after repairs are made, you'll be significantly slower, enough to cost you the race. Still, you can use the draft to salvage a decent finish.

OK, so you banged up that shiny car, but you weren't lucky enough to bring out the caution. Should you pit? I don't know.

If you pit under green, you're going to lose at least a lap, probably two. If you haven't sustained wheel damage, you should consider staying out and hope for a caution. You might be able to hold off the cars behind you and stay in the lead lap. Of course, you might get lapped on the track, and then have to pit under the green anyway. Hey, that's why you get paid the big bucks!

Sears Point

Let's face it: road racing is the true test of driving skill. The ovals have their own demands: intense focus, sharp judgment, lightning-quick reactions, nerves of steel, and cajones of titanium. But the road circuits demand an athlete's sense of timing and a knowledge of the track that borders on obsession. This game doesn't make it easy. It faithfully models the cars and the tracks, and models how those cars behave on those tracks. There's no magic to turning decent laps here. You just have to practice until you know this track like you know your way to the bathroom. And then you have to get around it fast. So this is why they pay those Formula One guys the really big bucks.

Track Statistics

Length	2.52 miles
Lap record	91.838 (Dale Earnhardt)
Full fuel run	25–30 laps

Race Length Options

100%	227 miles	90 laps	2 stops
80%	181 miles	72 laps	2 stops
60%	136 miles	54 laps	1 stop
50%	113 miles	45 laps	1 stop
40%	91 miles	36 laps	1 stop

Figure 6.17
This twisting course in the California hills is a true test of your driving skills. In other words, it's really hard.

SET-UP

Car set-up isn't the key to getting around the road courses—it's your driving ability. You can run fast enough to win with the stock Ace set-up, but here are a few general tips. "Neutral" is the word here. You'll be turning both ways, so the tricks you use to get the car to turn left easily on the ovals are useless here. You want stagger set to zero and as much rear spoiler as you can get. Shift the weight bias slightly to the ride side, since there are more right-hand turns here. Follow Geoff Bodine's advice in the manual for shock settings: the softer the better at Sears Point.

You may find the car more comfortable to drive if you decrease the wheel-lock setting. There are plenty of tight turns at Sears Point, so experiment to find the lowest setting that gets you through those corners comfortably.

Gearing is more important here than on the good ol' boy ovals since—you guessed it—you're constantly shifting on the road courses. There are four corners at Sears Point that you'll negotiate at 50 mph or less, so you have to pay attention to the ratios in all four gears, including first. During pre-season practice, work those slow corners extensively to see what RPMs

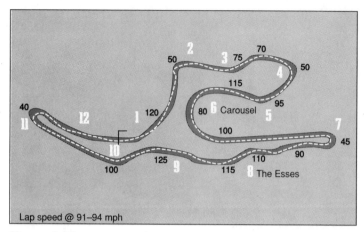

Lap speed @ 91–94 mph

Figure 6.18

you're pulling through them. Adjust the first-gear ratio so that you don't have to shift into second until you're exiting the turns.

The nuances of chassis set-up don't mean anything until you learn your way around the track. Don't even bother to adjust the car until you learn the proper line through the turns.

THE GROOVE

Of course, there is no single, magic groove around Sears Point. Each turn is different, requiring different entrance and exit lines. See Chapter 3 for some general tips on driving road courses, and study the track graphic shown here. Above all else, practice. Then practice some more. Keep the track graphic handy as you're practicing, so you'll know at all times where you are on the track, and what turn you're approaching next.

PASSING

You'll find passing a tall order at Sears Point. Like other road courses, most passes are made under braking on approach to a turn. Work for inside position and just drive a little deeper into the turn than the other guy, and then stand on the brakes.

The two short straightaways provide a brief chance to pass, but the key is hitting the right line and getting traction off the previous corner, so that you have the speed headed down the straight.

In 1991 Sears Point was the scene of one of the most controversial moments in NASCAR racing. On the final lap, Davey Allison was leading, with Ricky Rudd, one of the circuit's best road racers, right on his bumper. As the two racers approached the final turn—the hairpin leading to the start-finish line—the cars bumped and Allison's Ford spun out of control. Rudd streaked alone toward the checkered flag. • It wasn't a checkered flag that greeted Rudd, however; it was a black flag. NASCAR ruled that Rudd bumped Allison intentionally to win the race. Rudd and others—including Dave Marcis, who was running just behind the two—claimed Allison had driven into the turn too hard and was already out of control when Rudd bumped him. NASCAR officials disagreed, and Allison was awarded the victory.

PIT STRATEGY

OK, so you really stink at Sears Point. That doesn't mean you can't salvage a top-10 finish. Try to stretch your pit stops as far as possible. Tires shouldn't be a problem, so keep a close eye on your fuel mileage. Use the gas mileage data here as a starting point, but remember, that number varies wildly on the road courses, depending on your driving style and how fast you're getting around the track. Oh, and don't run out of gas. It may be a long way back to the pits.

If you bang up your car on one of those twisting turns, don't pit unless wheel damage forces you in. You run pretty slow here, so a little dent isn't going to slow you down.

Charlotte

The Charlotte Motor Speedway is a jewel on the NASCAR circuit. With its luxury condos, fine dining, and sparkling

Figure 6.19
Jeff Gordon leads a
tight pack through
turn 1 at Charlotte.

amenities, CMS is racing's answer to Disney World. It's a nice
place, all right, but it can be a frightening track to drive at 180
mph. Close racing and plenty of passing makes Charlotte one
of the most thrilling stops on the schedule.

Track Statistics

Length	1.5 miles
Banking	24 degrees
Lap record	185.759 (Ward Burton)
Full fuel run	65–70 laps

Race Length Options

SPRING RACE (600 miles)

100%	600 miles	400 laps	5 stops
80%	480 miles	320 laps	4 stops
60%	360 miles	240 laps	3 stops
50%	300 miles	200 laps	2 stops?
40%	240 miles	160 laps	2 stops

Race Length Options

FALL RACE (500 miles)

100%	500 miles	333 laps	4 stops?
80%	400 miles	267 laps	3 stops?
60%	300 miles	200 laps	2 stops?
50%	250 miles	167 laps	2 stops
40%	200 miles	133 laps	1 stop?

SET-UP

Charlotte requires both speed in the straightaways and grip in the corners, so your set-up must reflect that compromise. Start with the Ace set-up (which is quick enough to outrun computer drivers at 100%), and then play with the rear spoiler to see how much downforce you need to stick to the bottom of the track through the corners. Reduce the angle a degree or two, then see if you can still drive it deep into the turns. Find a spoiler setting that gives you top speed at the end of the straightaways—190+ mph—but still gives you enough downforce to keep the car stable in the turns.

Be careful not to limit your top speed with a gear ratio that's too high. As you learn the track, you'll be able to drive deeper into the corners, so make sure you leave some extra RPMs at the top end of the gearing to allow yourself a bit of room to get better. If you find that you're able to stay on the gas longer, you might over-rev the engine if the gear ratio is too high.

THE GROOVE

Charlotte features a wide racing groove that makes for plenty of side-by-side action. The quickest line through the corners begins with a high entrance. From near the top of the track, drive the car down near the grass as you reach the apex at both ends of the speedway. As usual, let the car climb back up the track and out toward the wall as you exit the turns. Once the tires get warmed up, you should be able to go through the corners close to 160 mph.

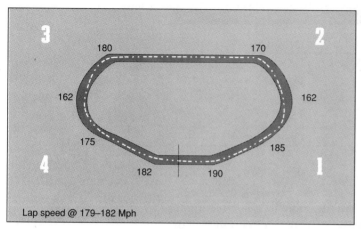

Lap speed @ 179–182 Mph

Figure 6.20

These are high-speed corners, and that makes for a tricky transition from turn 4 to the front stretch and its two doglegs. You negotiate the doglegs the same way: Take the car up against the wall as you approach, and then cut down to the grass in the middle of the dogleg. Your goal is to turn the front straightaway into one long, sweeping curve leading into turn 1. Take it easy through here until you get some heat in the tires, because the car wants to break loose coming off turn 4.

Unless you're running in heavy traffic or get into a corner too hard, you shouldn't have to get on the brakes here. As you reach the entrance to the turns, roll out of the throttle gently to bring the speed down from 190 mph to about 180 mph. Let the turn scrub off the rest of the speed you'll need to get through the turn.

PASSING

Every lap at Charlotte can be an adventure, even when you're the only car on the track. Put 38 other cars out there, and it can get hairy. Fortunately, there are plenty of passing opportunities around this speedway.

The backstretch is long enough to use the draft to blow by one or two cars. If you can't clear a car before you reach turn

3, don't worry. The middle of the track is the preferred line into the corner, but the low groove works well, too. Go ahead and drive it in there, maybe letting off the gas just a split-second sooner than you normally would. Get back on the throttle as soon as you can, and you can usually pull off the pass.

The doglegs on the frontstretch are another good passing opportunity. If you can get a good run off turn 4, you can pull alongside the lead car as you approach the first dogleg. The outside car can pull more RPMs on the on the high side of the track, but you should be able to stay beside it through the first dogleg, then cut across the second dogleg to complete the pass.

Because the fast line through the corners start with a high entrance, you can also pull off an outside pass, especially coming off turn 2. Watch out, though, because these guys will ride you right into the wall.

PIT STRATEGY

Very aggressive driving will abuse the right-front tire, but a more conservative—but still competitive—strategy will stretch the tires for a full run on gas. As always, be flexible with your gas strategy. If you're leading and the entire field comes in during a caution for tires and fuel, you'd better do the same. But if you're running 37th, you might want to roll the dice and to stay out to gain the positions. As a general rule, if you're running with the leaders at Charlotte, it doesn't pay to gamble on pit stops.

Dover Downs

As the name implies, Dover Downs doubles as a horse race track, and a few drivers might prefer to try their luck with the ponies here. They don't call it the Monster Mile for nothin'. A 500-mile race here is usually the longest race on the schedule, sometimes lasting nearly five hours. Dover is fast, tight, and unforgiving. Hit the wall here and you won't soon forget it—*if* you can remember it, that is.

Track Statistics

Length	1 mile
Banking	24 degrees
Lap record	152.840 (Geoff Bodine)
Full fuel run	110–115 laps

Race Length Options

100%	500 miles	500 laps	4 stops
80%	400 miles	400 laps	3 stops
60%	300 miles	300 laps	2 stops
50%	250 miles	250 laps	2 stops
40%	200 miles	200 laps	1 stop

SET-UP

Pure horsepower takes a back seat to handling on this demanding one-mile oval. Once you locate the precise line around Dover, the Ace set-up is fast enough to run with the leaders. But you want to dominate, don't you?

The right-front tire is your enemy here. Push the car too hard and you'll burn that tire right off the rim. You know the story. The tire builds up heat, it loses grip, and the car pushes up the race track, which heats the tire even more. Try a softer shock to ease the pressure on the right-front. The car won't be quite as responsive coming off the turns, but you should be able to cool the tire slightly.

From the Ace set-up, change the fourth-gear ratio one step shorter. That will give you greater top-end speed at the end of the straightaway. Watch out, though; you'll have to adjust your braking point to compensate for the faster entry into the corner.

Figure 6.21
Single-file racing is the norm at the brutal one-mile speedway in Delaware.

THE GROOVE

First, the good news. Dover is a true oval, with symmetrical turns, so the line through the corners are identical at both ends of the speedway. Now, the bad news. Dover is a one-groove race track. Stray out of the narrow line and you'll scrub off speed in a hurry, and watch the leaders pull away and disappear.

Turn into the corner from about the middle of the race track, and then drive the car down to the bottom groove. You have to use quite a bit of brakes getting into the corners, but remember: easy does it. Don't slam on the brakes; apply brakes gently to bring your speed down to 145 mph or so. As your cornering speed drops below 140 mph, roll back into the throttle, feathering the gas to keep the car on the edge of control. You need to be at full throttle just past the apex of the turn.

PASSING

Dover resembles a really fast short track, with lots of braking and an emphasis on holding the low groove through the corners. That makes for tough passing, so be patient as you try to work your way through the field. Passing here is usually done one car at a time.

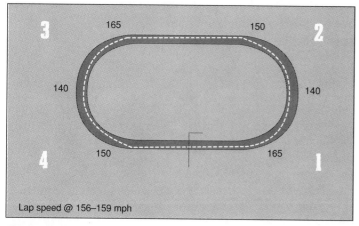

Figure 6.22

Dover may be a one-groove race track in this simulation, but in real life, two of the sport's greatest drivers were able to carve out their own groove to tame the Monster Mile. • Richard Petty and Harry Gant won several races at the Dover mile by driving their cars where few drivers dared to tread: the high groove. While other racers would stick to the established—and safer—low line, Petty and Gant found a quick line at the top of the track. • Running right up against the wall through the turns, Petty and "High Groove" Harry proved that Dover can be conquered by running at the top of the track. Can *you* find the high groove?

It's tough to pull off a clean pass on these short straightaways. Even if you get a good run off the corner and pull alongside the lead car, you'll usually have to finish off the pass through the next turn. The inside is the preferred position, but the faster entry is slightly up the track. When you get inside the lead car on the straightaway, try to force the other car up the race track so that you won't be forced to enter the corner on the bottom of the track.

As on the short tracks, the safest way to pass a competitive car is to follow it closely through the turns and wait for the other driver to slip up the track.

PIT STRATEGY

Since passing is so difficult here, pit strategy is often the key to a good finish. Unless you're really smooth, the punishment given to the right-front tire won't allow you to make a full fuel run. If the race stays green, let the right front be the determining factor when deciding when to pit. Use the F5 key often to monitor tire wear, and be ready to pit when the tire-wear indicator turns red.

Consider pitting during just about every yellow flag, depending, of course, on your track position. If the caution period is followed by a long green-flag run, you'll be glad you have a fresh right-front tire.

Pocono

This triangular speedway, nestled in Pennsylvania's Pocono mountains, is in a class by itself on the NASCAR circuit. Part superspeedway, part road course, and part short track, Pocono is a riddle to many race teams. It's a tough track to figure out, but Pocono provides some of the most exciting racing on the tour.

Track Statistics

Length	2.5 miles
Banking, turn 1	14 degrees
Banking, turn 2	8 degrees
Banking, turn 3	6 degrees
Lap record	185.830 (Greg Sacks)
Full fuel run	40–45 lap

Race Length Options			
100%	500 miles	200 laps	4 stops
80%	400 miles	160 laps	3 stops
60%	300 miles	120 laps	2 stops
50%	250 miles	100 laps	2 stops
40%	200 miles	80 laps	1 stop

SET-UP

The Pocono tri-oval is a stern challenge for both drivers and mechanics. Nowhere else will you have to negotiate 190 mph straightaways followed by 130 mph corners. And none of the three corners is the same. Turn 1 is sharper than 2 or 3, while 2 and 3 are much flatter. Setting up a car to work well here, then, is a compromise. Don't sweat if you can't find the perfect Pocono set-up—the real experts are still looking for it, too.

You're hunting for the ideal combination of straightaway speed and cornering ability. Start with the Ace set-up, but you can do better. To pick up a few mph on the straightaways, lower the rear spoiler from 70 degrees to 60 degrees. The lower spoiler will take a bit of downforce of the rear end, but you can compensate by increasing the cross weight to +50 pounds. Now you'll be faster on both the straightaways and in the corners. Keep an eye on the right-front tire temperatures, since that extra weight on the left rear is transferred to the right front in a corner.

If you're shifting here—and you should be—try a taller ratio for third gear. Watch your RPMs at the end of the straightaway leading to turn 3. If you're red-lining the tach well before you back off and begin braking, a taller ratio will ease wear on the engine and give you more room for acceleration.

THE GROOVE

Ah, the groove at Pocono! It depends on which groove you're talking about. Like a road course, the each turn at Pocono is unique, and requires its own line.

Figure 6.23
High-speed straightaways lead into flat, treacherous corners at Pocono.

Enter turn 1 near the bottom on the track and keep the low line—with your left-side wheels on or near the red-and-white curbing—all the way through the corner. You want to get into turn 2 much higher on the race track, and then cut down toward the lower-middle groove as you round the apex. Turn 3 also requires a high entrance, followed by a sweeping line that carries the car toward the bottom groove as you exit onto the straightaway.

In recent years, NASCAR drivers have begun shifting gears at Pocono, and the same tactic will work for you. Downshifting for the corners will help you slow from the 190-mph straightaways, and it will give you greater acceleration coming off the turns.

As you approach turn 1, lightly apply the brakes to slow the car to within about 140 mph, and then shift into third gear just before you steer into the turn. Keep it in third until you shift into fourth headed down the next straightaway. You get into turn 2 the same way, except it's a much faster turn. As you exit turn 2, however, you can leave the shifter in third gear all the way down that short straightaway and into turn 3.

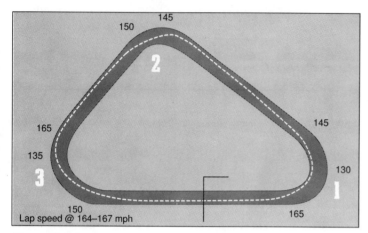

Figure 6.24

PASSING

If you've learned the quick route around Pocono, then passing should be no problem. There's a lot of straightaway here, so the draft plays an important role. Practice getting through the turns without losing ground, and then use the draft—and your horsepower advantage over the computer cars—to blow past the lead cars. You can pass several cars on one straight, but you'll probably want to get back into line before you reach these flat, tight turns.

Passing in the turns is a bit trickier. It's a lot like short-tracking racing, except you're under heavy braking down from 180–190 mph. The car is very unstable under these conditions, so bold moves with the steering wheel can get you into trouble. Outbrake your opponent as you enter the turn, and then look for an opening on the inside through the apex. If you're good, you can pull it off.

PIT STRATEGY

Think twice before you gamble on fuel mileage at Pocono. At 2.5 miles, with relatively slow average speeds, this place is unforgiving if you guess wrong. Run out of gas here and you probably can't coast to the pits.

Even with the risks, many races have been won here on fuel mileage. Long green-flag runs are common at Pocono, so stretching your mileage into one fewer stop than your opponents can win the race. Just make sure you're right when you make your calculations.

Michigan

Michigan International Speedway is a racer's dream. The track is wide, smooth, roomy—and plenty fast. Cars scramble for position three- and four-wide while topping 200 mph. For pure entertainment, this may be the premier speedway on the circuit.

Track Statistics

Length	2 miles
Banking	18 degrees
Lap record	181.082 (Geoff Bodine)
Full fuel run	50–55 laps

Race Length Options

100%	400 miles	200 laps	3 stops
80%	320 miles	160 laps	3 stops
60%	240 miles	120 laps	2 stops
50%	200 miles	100 laps	1 stop
40%	160 miles	80 laps	1 stop

Figure 6.25
Michigan's wide, smooth track is the site of some of the most exciting racing on the tour.

TIP

Michigan was "repaved" for Version 1.2 of the game. If you're running 1.0 or 1.1, get the new version from Papyrus or download it from one of the on-line services. You'll be in for a pleasant surprise. The new racing surface is much faster and has better grip.

SET-UP

The Ace set-up will get you around Michigan in good shape, but you can tweak the set-up for a little more speed. First knock the rear spoiler down to 65 degrees. You'll pick up a couple of miles per hour and the car should still be stable through the turns. You can afford a shorter ratio in fourth gear, so bump that up to 3.50. You should now be able to top 200 mph at the end of the straightaways.

Despite the high-speed turns, the right-front tire doesn't take much punishment here, so try stiffening the right-front shock to make the car more responsive. You might also try

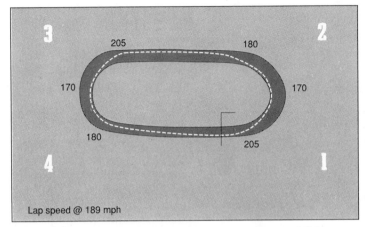

Figure 6.26

shifting some weight to the rear of the car, as much as 50% or more. The car will be a bit looser, but you should be able to corner faster.

THE GROOVE

There are several lines to run at Michigan, but you'll get around here quickest by entering the turns high on the race track, and then sweeping down to the bottom groove through the turns.

Run the car right up to the outside wall down the backstretch, and then cut left down the track as you enter turn 3. Ride the low line through turns 3 and 4, and then let your momentum carry the car high up on the banking as you exit four and head for the slight dogleg on the frontstretch. You can run low toward the dogleg, but the faster line is on the outside. Square up the car alongside the outside wall as you approach turn 1.

You should be able to stay off the brakes, except when you're driving in traffic. And you can drive the car deeper into the turns than you may first think, especially going into turn 1. Get used to rolling out of the throttle just as you enter the turns, and then see if you can hold the gas down just a little longer. Overdriving into the turns, however, will scrub off speed and reduce your exit speed off the corner.

PASSING

The beauty of Michigan is its many passing lanes. Racing here often looks like rush-hour traffic on the freeway, with cars running three and four abreast. Only here, that traffic jam is screaming along at 190 mph.

The straightaways are long enough for lots of passing, and the draft is very much in play. You can also pass in the corners at both ends of the speedway, inside or outside.

The most fun place to pass, though, is through the dogleg down the frontstretch. The preferred line as you approach the dogleg is the middle of the track and above, but if you get a good run off the fourth turn, you can drive up alongside a car on the low side of the track. Then it's a drag race to turn 1. If you catch a car running low out of turn 4, then take the high side of the track and pass him on the outside as you head for the start/finish line.

PIT STRATEGY

There typically aren't many cautions on this speedway, so a 400-mile race here can go by quickly. Assume this race will stay green, and plan on making the 400 miles on three stops. Tire wear shouldn't be a factor, so stretch your fuel as far as you can.

If you're a gas-mileage gambler, Michigan is a pretty good place to bet. The cars usually stays bunched up here, and if you're fast you can fly through the field in a hurry. So if you've run 20 or 30 laps and a caution flag comes out, think about pitting for tires and fuel. You'll lose some positions, but you might gain a lot more if you can delay or avoid a green-flag stop later on.

Loudon

The good ol' boys come north once a year to New England to race on this beautiful one-mile speedway. Loudon is fast and

Figure 6.27
Loudon's flat turns demand patience. Keep the pressure on the car ahead and wait for the driver to make a mistake.

flat, a stern test of a driver's ability to handle a race car. Get ready to fight each lap to stay in control and keep the car pointed in the right direction. Welcome to flat-track racing.

Track Statistics

Length	1.058 miles
Banking	12 degrees
Lap record	127.197 (Ernie Irvan)
Full fuel run	100–110 laps

Race Length Options

100%	317 miles	300 laps	2 stops
80%	254 miles	240 laps	2 stops
60%	190 miles	180 laps	1 stop
50%	159 miles	150 laps	1 stop
40%	127 miles	120 laps	1 stop

SET-UP

The Ace set-up that came with the game is pretty fast here, good enough to run up front if you can hit the lines and run consistent

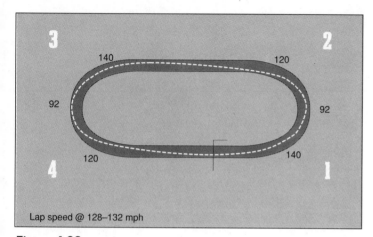

Lap speed @ 128–132 mph

Figure 6.28

laps. Here are a couple of ideas that might squeeze a bit more speed out of that set-up, depending on your driving style.

A loose car can be faster at Loudon—if you can handle it, that is. After you get comfortable running the track, try decreasing the cross-weight to loosen up the chassis a little. At first, the car will be a bear to drive. But after the tires heat up, and you get accustomed to keeping the car headed in a straight lines off the turns, you'll be faster.

To help combat this loose condition, try stiffening the right-side shocks, perhaps to 90%. Despite the slipping and sliding you do here, the tires shouldn't get excessively hot.

As usual, you can shorten the ratio of fourth gear to turn a little more RPMs at the end of the straightaways.

THE GROOVE

They call Loudon "the Miracle Mile," and I'm not sure why. Maybe because it's a miracle if you can get more than a few laps around here without spinning out or slapping the wall. Outside of the road courses, Loudon and its evil cousin, Phoenix, are the toughest tracks on the circuit.

The conventional line around Loudon is one that takes you to the outside down the straightaways, entering the corners high on the track, and then cutting across the turn so that you're running at the bottom through the apex. You can get through the corners on this line at 110 mph or more.

You can hit 160 mph or more at the end of the straightaways, so you'll need plenty of brakes to get the car slowed to make the turn. Once you've slowed and turned into the corner, get back on the gas, feathering the throttle so that you can reach full acceleration as soon as possible.

The challenge here is to keep the car from sliding out of control as you exit the turns. The transition from the 14-degree banking of the turns to the flat straightaways makes the car want to break loose even more.

A faster—and definitely more daring—line is the one shown in the diagram. In this groove, you enter the turns high and you stay high. Drift dangerously close to the wall in the middle of the turn, and then cut back across the track under acceleration exiting the corner. You'll have to slow to about 90 mph in the middle of the turn, much slower than the conventional line. But you'll more than make up for that lack of speed as you come off the turn. Because the car isn't turning as tightly on the outside of the curve, the chassis will respond better to acceleration and the tires won't lose grip.

PASSING

The best place to make a pass at Loudon is: anywhere you can. Actually, it's classic short-track passing. Get a fender up alongside the other fellow coming out of a turn or down the straightaway, and then outbrake him—or outmuscle him—through the next corner.

The trick is to get inside position, and then be able to squeeze enough speed out of the car in the bottom groove. The car tends to be loose here anyway, and it's tougher to get traction at the bottom of the track coming off the turns. If you can't get a good grip on the inside, try drifting higher, perhaps even nudging the car on the outside to let the other guy know you're there. Remember, stock-car racing is a contact sport.

If you can find the high groove shown in the track graphic, you won't have to worry too much about passing, because you'll have that line all to yourself. You'll lose ground in the middle of the corners, but you should be able to catch and pass the lead car with your greater exit speed.

PIT STRATEGY

Because passing is such a chore on this flat, unforgiving race track, you might want to play your fuel-mileage card here. Drive fairly conservatively and you can coax enough wear out of the tires to last a full fuel stop. If you're having trouble running up front here—and most players do—try to outsmart 'em in the pits.

Watkins Glen

Ah, another road course! Just what the doctor ordered after wrestling your 3,800-pound car around Loudon for a few hours. Watkins Glen is one of America's most storied racing facilities, and also one of the country's most challenging. It's plenty fast, and the combination of high speeds and tight turns is perhaps the toughest test you'll find on the circuit. If you can win here, consider yourself a racer.

Track Statistics

Length	2.454 miles
Lap record	120.411 (Mark Martin)
Full fuel run	30–35 laps

Race Length Options

100%	221 miles	90 laps	2 stops
80%	177 miles	72 laps	2 stops
60%	132 miles	54 laps	1 stop
50%	110 miles	45 laps	1 stop
40%	88 miles	36 laps	1 stop

Figure 6.29
You'd better finish that pass down the back-stretch before you reach the chicane at historic Watkins Glen.

SET-UP

As you surely realize by now, chassis set-up isn't the key to running well at the road courses. The Ace set-up is plenty fast to win, as long as you know how to get around these fast and dangerous turns.

After you get friendly with this track, you might want to play around with a few settings. All the tough turns are right-handers, so try shifting a little weight to the ride side by decreasing the left bias. Experiment with shock settings, too, stiffening the left side since it absorbs most of the punishment in the corners.

One adjustment you can make immediately is the gearing. Shorten the stock gearing in the Ace set-up by one or two steps in fourth gear to increase your straightaway speed.

THE GROOVE

Watkins Glen is a tough place to figure out, a challenge that's complicated by the high-speed turns. See Chapter 3 for some road-racing tips, but one tip is worth repeating here. *Slow down to go faster*. I know, it sounds dumb, but the key to getting around a road course is how well you negotiate the entrance to the turns. If you're too hot getting into the turn, you'll slide out of the groove and screw up your exit line, which reduces

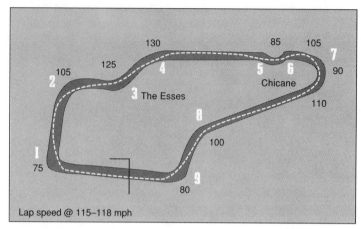

Figure 6.30

your speed headed down the next straight, and so on. One bad entrance can ruin half a lap, not to mention that pretty new paint job.

PASSING

Unlike Sears Point, this course has enough straightaway to allow some clean passes. Your best bet is on the backstretch coming off turn 3. Just make sure you clear the lead car before you get to the chicane, or you'll both be in trouble. The second straightaway, called the short chute, affords less of a passing opportunity. But if you can grab the preferred line—to the left— headed into the next turn, you might be able to pull it off. The same is true for the front stretch through the start/finish line. Get to the inside—the right side this time—and try to outbrake the other guy into turn 1, the slowest corner on the track.

PIT STRATEGY

Track position is your priority at Watkins Glen, so you should play your pit strategy with that in mind. If you're running near the front, take your cue from the leaders, pitting when they do. If you're running at the back of the pack, pit at every opportunity for fresh tires and a full tank of gas. You're going to need every advantage you can find.

Phoenix

Since the demise of the tracks in Riverside and Ontario, California, this desert raceway is the westernmost stop for the NASCAR boys. Phoenix is also one of the most difficult stops on the tour. Very similar to the tough-as-nails mile at Loudon, this tri-oval is relatively flat, demanding smooth driving, braking, and acceleration.

Track Statistics

Length	1 mile
Banking	11 degrees
Lap record	129.833 (Sterling Marlin)
Full fuel run	100–110 laps

Race Length Options

100%	312 miles	312 laps	2 stops
80%	250 miles	250 laps	2 stops
60%	187 miles	187 laps	1 stops
50%	156 miles	156 laps	1 stop
40%	125 miles	125 laps	1 stop

SET-UP

Fast laps at Phoenix require a loose set-up, and the stock Ace settings will work well enough to run with the leaders. If you can handle the car, though, a little looser might be a little faster. Try increasing the rear bias slightly, to a little more than 50%. Reduce cross weight slightly, to about +0. *Now* we're talking loose. If you can drive it this way, you'll be plenty fast enough to win.

You should be able to get good tire wear at Phoenix, so experiment with the shocks, increasing their stiffness to make the car more responsive in traffic.

Figure 6.31
Cars fight for track position at Phoenix as they negotiate the tricky backstretch dogleg.

THE GROOVE

Enter turn 1 toward the middle of the track. Drive the car slightly lower on the track as you round the apex, but you don't want to go to the bottom groove. You'll come off turn 1 lower than you entered, and then swing out near the wall to line up for the dogleg on the backstretch. Cut the dogleg close, almost clipping the grass on the inside. Head down the short straightaway toward turn 3 almost in the middle of the track, and then drift up to make your entrance into the turn fairly high on the track. Try to keep the car low as you accelerate off turn 4 and onto the front straightaway.

After winning his first NASCAR race at Phoenix in 1989, an overjoyed Alan Kulwicki created a bit of racing lore. The delirious Kulwicki promptly drove around the track counter-clockwise, his fist pumping out the window in celebration. Victory laps are a tradition in racing, but driving the wrong way on the track isn't. Kulwicki called it his Polish victory lap. After his death in 1992, several of his fellow drivers honored their colleague with their own Polish victory laps after scoring wins.

You'll need to get on the brakes pretty hard, especially getting into the very tight turn 1. Again, brake firmly but smoothly.

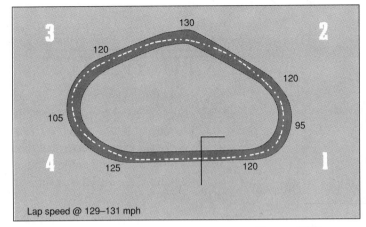

130
120
120
105
95
4
125
120
1
Lap speed @ 129–131 mph

Figure 6.32

Slamming on the brakes will just throw the car sideways, and that's no way to enter the turns here.

PASSING

Acceleration coming off the corners is the key to pulling off a pass at Phoenix, and that means you have to be as smooth as silk getting into the corners. If you can gain on the lead car coming off turn 4, then you might be able to get a fender alongside as you head toward turn 1. Be careful, though, going through turn 1 on the inside of another car. It's hard to keep the car low through the corner, so the momentum tends to push you up the track and into the outside car. You'll have to get out of the gas sooner to keep the car on the bottom of turn 1, and that usually allows the other car to beat you off the corner.

It's possible to pass through the backstretch dogleg, but it requires a good line and plenty of speed coming off turn 2. If you have enough acceleration, pull to the inside and try to clip the infield grass as you cross the dogleg. Watch out for the car on the outside. They like to run you into the grass here.

Turns 3 and 4 are probably the best passing opportunities on the track. If you're comfortable taking the high line through this corner, then an outside pass is your best bet. If you prefer the low groove, try to carry the outside car higher than he'd like, and then cut down the track as you go through turn 4.

PIT STRATEGY

Like all tracks where passing is so difficult, you can improve your finish at Phoenix by stretching your mileage and using yellow flags to make pit stops. If you can't keep up with the leaders, then focus on staying in the lead lap and pitting as little as possible under the green. On the other hand, when the yellow flag flies, dive into the pits for fresh rubber and a full tank.

GETTING THE MOST OUT OF NASCAR RACING

Technical Stuff

TO GET THE MOST ENJOYMENT FROM *NASCAR RACING*, YOU NEED TO work on more than your driving skills and your car set-ups. The program gives you a bevy of choices to make the game more to your liking. Let's look at the standard options, plus a few trickier adjustments you can make.

IN SEARCH OF FRAME RATE

Let's face it: There isn't a PC in the world that will run *NASCAR Racing* at its highest frame rate with all the graphics turned on. The next generation of processors might do it, but this is an incredibly CPU-intensive simulation. Until you get that dream machine, you have some hard choices to make. Actually, it's an easy choice: get the fastest frame rate possible from your machine, even if it means sacrificing those lovely graphics.

FRAME RATE VERSUS GRAPHICS

I began playing *NASCAR Racing* on a 486/33 machine, and I've since stepped up to a Pentium 90, and then a Pentium 133. Being a game reviewer and all, I have to keep pace with the cutting-edge games, right? And nobody would be foolish enough to spend thousands of dollars just to run *NASCAR Racing* better, would they? Of course not.

Frame rate is a measurement of performance, and in real-time, high-speed games like racing sims and flight sims, it makes all the difference. Like cartoon animations, computer games consist of a series of still "pictures" that are drawn and that advance so quickly as to create the illusion of motion. The faster those graphics are drawn, the smoother the animation.

In *NASCAR Racing*, frame rate isn't just a convenience, and its importance isn't only to make the game look better. Playing the game with a slow frame rate is like driving in a time warp. Your split-second reactions are translated a split-second later in the game, and that delay makes controlling the car even more

Figure 7.1
NASCAR Racing
looks stunningly
realistic with all
the graphics
options turned
on. Trouble is,
you can't run it
that way.

difficult. When you're sailing into turn 1 at Michigan at 200 mph with cars all around you, that can spell disaster.

NASCAR Racing is tough enough when it's running well. Don't make it harder by running at a slow frame rate when you can avoid it.

FINDING THE RIGHT FRAME RATE

There are programs available to measure frame rate, but *NASCAR Racing* has a tool that will help you get the most out of the game on your system. In the Graphics section under the Game Options menu, you can set various graphic elements to On, Off, or Auto. You'll also find settings for Minimum and Maximum Frame Rate. When the graphic elements are set to Auto, the game will toggle those graphics on and off to maintain the Minimum Frame Rate you choose. The highest setting is 30, and that's where you need to be. You can try a lower setting to accommodate a favorite graphic element, but if you go below about 20, you're going to be hard-pressed to drive the car competitively, especially in traffic.

We'll look at a couple of hardware configurations below, but you can use this feature to optimize the game for any computer. Set Minimum Frame Rate to 30 and all the separate graphic elements to Auto. Now go to a single race—any track will do—and see which graphic extras are turned on. If there

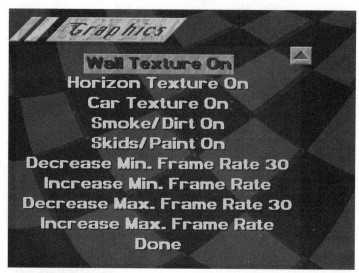

Graphics

> Wall Texture On
> Horizon Texture On
> Car Texture On
> Smoke/Dirt On
> Skids/Paint On
> Decrease Min. Frame Rate 30
> Increase Min. Frame Rate
> Decrease Max. Frame Rate 30
> Increase Max. Frame Rate
> Done

Figure 7.2
Don't be afraid to turn off some of the optional graphics. If you can't get a smooth frame rate, pretty graphics won't matter.

are none, then you're not going to reach 30 in your current configuration, but at least you'll know your machine is running at the fastest rate it can.

Now exit back to the Graphics menu under Options. Turn Car Textures to Auto, and then go back to the same track and see what you get. If the Car Textures remain on as you drive down the pit road, you've got a start. Go back to Graphics and switch Car Textures from Auto to On. Keep adding graphic elements, one by one, in the same way until you reach your machine's limit.

PIT STOP

Here's my graphics wish list, in descending order of importance:

- Car texture (a must)
- Skids/paint (you need 'em to drive)
- Object detail (love those signs)
- Smoke/dirt (nicer-looking wrecks)
- Wall texture (cool stuff)
- Horizon texture (forget it; you're not sightseeing, buddy)
- Grandstand texture (lose the crowds; they're just slowing you down)
- Grass texture (don't need it)
- Asphalt texture (you kidding? wait 'til you get a 786/200 machine)

If you can run the game in SVGA mode (more on that in a minute) but lack the hardware to run the extra graphics, then don't worry about all the bells and whistles. Heck, they'll just distract you, anyway. Just turn Car Textures On and go for it.

Personally, I can't stand graphics flashing in and out in the Auto mode. Crowds popping in and out of the grandstand are distracting and not realistic, at least in my world. Use the Auto mode and the frame rate settings to find an acceptable blend of graphics and frame rate, and then turn the graphics that run comfortably to the On position.

INCREASING FRAME RATE

There are a few tricks you can try to increase frame rate. Don't expect dramatic improvements, but by adjusting several of these settings, you will see a substantial improvement in performance. So if you really want to put the fans back in the grandstand, here's how.

NUMBER OF COMPETITORS

Limiting the number of competitors is your most powerful tool within the game to enhance the graphics while maintaining frame rate. Your computer has to constantly calculate every movement of every one of these cars. With 39 cars on the track, that's a lot of numbers-crunching.

I hate to leave drivers out of a race, but there's a good rationale for reducing the number of opponents from 38 to 28 or 30. While 39 cars start the races on the larger tracks, the field for short-track races is reduced to as few as 28 cars, at Richmond. The drivers don't compete for those starting spots. Instead, the same cars are always left out of the short-track races—the ones at the end of the line as you look at the cars in the Paint Kit or in the Driver Info section of the game.

Since these drivers can't run for the championship anyway—since they won't start several races—think about cutting them out of the action altogether. Reduce the number of opponents for all races to the lowest common denominator, 27 (28, counting you). That's not fair to those hard-working drivers and crews, but, hey, you've got frame rate to think about.

Figure 7.3
The number of
opponents drawn
in front of you has
an impact on
overall frame
rate, but you'll
want to see pretty
far ahead.

NUMBER OF CARS DRAWN

To tweak frame rate further, you can reduce the number of cars
that you actually see on the track. Go to Opponents in the
Options menu, and then lower the number of Opponents
Drawn in Front and Opponents Drawn Behind. This will
improve frame rate when it matters most—when there's heavy
traffic all around you.

Reduce the cars drawn in front from the default eight to
five or six, and see if this makes a noticeable difference. Be careful, though, because the fewer cars you can see ahead on the
track, the less time you'll have to react when there's trouble.
You may not see that car spinning up ahead.

What's happening behind you isn't nearly as important as
what's going on in front, so feel free to reduce this number to
two, maybe even one. You'll rarely have more than one car trying to pass at one time.

NUMBER OF CARS HEARD

The rumble of high-powered engines is a nice effect, but it does
nothing to help you drive, and it reduces frame rate. Try a setting of 2 or 3. You may not notice any difference, but remember, these changes are incremental and cumulative. Put
together, they might get you some more graphics without costing you any frame rate.

Figure 7.4
If you're running the game on a 486, you're stuck with the low-res graphics. Don't be blue: it's still a great game. And maybe Santa will bring you a Pentium for Christmas.

SOUND THINKING

When you start *NASCAR Racing* with the "Nascar" command, the program automatically loads digital sound. Sounds great, but it's costing you frame rate. If you're having trouble getting the game to run smoothly, try starting the program with a "- F" command extension. Typing "Nascar - fm" will force the game to run FM instead of digital sound, and the boost to frame rate can be significant. Tests run by Papyrus found that digital sound occupied as much as 20% of the processor's capacity.

SYSTEM CONFIGURATIONS

NASCAR Racing is one of the most demanding games—or software programs of any kind, for that matter—on the market today. The single most important factor is processor speed, but other factors impact how well the game runs, including the video card, video memory, and the amount of RAM in your machine.

486 MACHINES

If you're running *NASCAR Racing* on a 486 machine, you have to come to grips with a sad fact: this sim just isn't going to run in high-res SVGA mode. Officially, the minimum system to run high-res mode is a 486/66 MHz computer, but you won't be satisfied with the performance. It'll be just too choppy to drive.

Look on the bright side: the game looks fine in regular VGA mode, and it will run reasonably well on a 486/33, with most of the graphics options turned off. Just don't ruin the fun by seeing how much better it looks in high-res. You'll be compelled to rush out and upgrade to a Pentium machine.

You can use the same tricks to boost the game's performance on a 486 computer. The most cost-efficient upgrade is a video accelerator card, which we'll discuss below.

PENTIUM MACHINES

NASCAR Racing will run on a 486, but it really soars on a Pentium. You should be able to run the game in high-res mode on any Pentium, but you'll need a 90 MHz machine or better to get really smooth frame rate. And even on the fastest computers, you can't get all the graphics detail and maintain the highest frame rate at the same time.

MEMORY

System memory is probably the least of your concerns. Eight megabytes of RAM is all you need to get peak performance. With 4 MB, the game won't be able to load grass and asphalt textures, but you probably won't be turning those textures on, anyway. With 8 MB, you get it all. Beyond 8 MB, the only enhancement you'll see is the length of your video replays. If you're looking to upgrade your current system to go racing, don't worry about memory.

VIDEO CARDS

Outside of CPU speed, the video card has the greatest impact on how well *NASCAR Racing* runs on your machine. Video cards have memory, too, and the amount and type of memory have a significant impact on system performance.

Just about any machine purchased since 1994 probably came with a video card containing 1 MB of memory. If you have an older machine with only 512 K of video memory, you just found your bottleneck. By stepping up to a 1 MB or a 2 MB video card, you'll greatly enhance your racing experience. And it's a relatively inexpensive upgrade. A very good graphics accelerator will cost between $200 and $300, and the extra speed will be apparent.

Go with a 2 MB card if you can afford it. There are two primary types of video memory available: VRAM and DRAM. VRAM is faster and, naturally, more expensive. But the cost difference is slight. A 2 MB VRAM card will be a good investment if you're looking to boost graphics performance. You'll find that *NASCAR Racing* will run better—and so will other graphics-intensive programs and games, not to mention Windows.

In general, the more expensive a card is, the faster *NASCAR Racing* will run with it. But beware: many cards are designed to enhance Windows performance, and some of those do almost nothing for MS-DOS applications. There are a number of good DOS accelerators available, including the Diamond Stealth 64 and the ATI Mach 64.

A new generation of video accelerator cards promises an even bigger boost to performance. These so-called 3-D accelerator cards take a greater share of the graphics burden, freeing up the processor to perform faster calculations and speeding up the frame rate.

These cards should be available now from two companies: Creative Labs, and Diamond Multimedia. Although performance will probably differ slightly among the makes, you should see a dramatic boost with either one. Papyrus supports both cards, and has tweaked the game to take advantage of their capabilities.

IN CONTROL

You have two choices here: a joystick or a steering wheel/pedals set-up. The wheel and pedals are much more realistic, but they're also pretty expensive. OK, you can steer with the keyboard, too, but you won't be happy with that for long. Unless, of course, you get a kick out of destroying expensive machinery.

QUICK ON THE STICK

Any quality joystick will do the job, but you'll appreciate the flexibility of the multi-button sticks such as the Thrustmaster and the CH Flickstick Pro. The game allows you to assign the throttle, brakes, and shifter to any button, so you can configure the stick any way you like. A conventional two-button joystick also works well.

GET A WHEEL AND PEDALS

If you're serious about your computer racing, you're going to want the real thing eventually. How'd you like steering your car down to the video store with a Thrustmaster? Hey, it might be kind of fun, at that. But it ain't racin'. You won't be your best on the race track using a joystick for a steering wheel and a keyboard for brakes. Once you get the game running well on your machine, the best investment you can make in *NASCAR Racing* is a wheel and pedals set-up. Give this ultra-realistic simulation the controls it deserves. You might actually feel you have more precise control with a joystick. But the oh-my-god-I'm-driving-a-race-car thrill you get from working the wheel and pedals takes this game to another level.

You have at least two choices, and you're gonna have to fork over at least $130 or so. The less expensive Thrustmaster Formula T1 is a solid performer, but may not hold up well in the long run, subjected to the beating it takes wrestling these 3,500-pound cars around the track. A sturdier—and more expensive—alternative called the TSW wheel is available from a small company that you can contact in the Motorsports Forum on CompuServe. The Thrustmaster wheel is widely available at retail stores. You won't go wrong with either. The Cadillac of wheels is from Extreme Competition Controls.

All right, so *maybe* I feel a little silly sitting at my desk, driving like a madman. But at least I'm not wearing a fire suit and a full-faced helmet. Not yet.

IN THE DRIVER'S SEAT

With a joystick, you feel like you're playing a computer game. With a wheel and pedals, you feel like you're driving. That realism will make you a better racer, too.

Figure 7.5
Sideways at Richmond. With a steering wheel, you'll have a better chance to save it.

The steering wheel allows you to drive your way out of trouble on the race track. When the rear end loses traction—a loose condition—you can turn the wheel slightly in the direction of the spin to get the car straightened out, sometimes without lifting off the gas. You can do the same thing with a joystick, but it just doesn't feel as natural.

The gas and brake pedals add to the sense of being there, too, but they're even more effective at increasing your lap speeds. With the keyboard or a joystick button working as your pedals, the throttle and brakes are either all the way on or all the way off. There is no gradual application.

Gas and brake pedals, on the other hand, work exactly the same in the game as they do in your car. You can "roll" into and out of the throttle to get the precise amount of acceleration you need to come off the corners at top speed.

The same applies to the brakes. Instead of slamming on the brakes every time you touch the brake key, you can work the pedal to gently slow the car as you enter a turn.

GAME OPTIONS: HAVE FUN, BUT BE REAL

The real beauty of *NASCAR Racing* is its almost infinite flexibility. You control almost every aspect of the game, from the number of laps to the strength of your opponents, from making your car invincible to setting the season schedule.

You can set up the game so that you'll win every time out. Won't that be fun? Just set the opponents to 70% strength, make your car indestructible, and run 10-lap races. You'll start on the pole and lead every lap of every race on your way to the championship.

At the other extreme, you can run full-length races against top opponents without saving the game, running grueling three- or four-hour races in one sitting. And if you wreck the car, your crew will patch it up as best they can so you can run slowly around the track for a couple hundred miles, trying to gain a few championship points.

You probably won't want to take either of those extreme approaches. You want realism—this is not an arcade game— but you can't devote your entire life to a computer game. Well, you can, but your family won't like it. Let's look for a happy medium.

RACE LENGTH

Races in NASCAR's premier division have traditionally run 500 miles, or 500 laps on tracks of less than one mile in length. That's a long haul, usually at least three hours, and sometimes more than four. I want realism, but I just don't have time to run 500-mile races. Heck, sometimes I have to play other games.

Remember, though, that as you shorten the length of the races, you also rob the sport of some of its strategy—when to pit and what to do when you pit. These cars usually run about 100 miles on a full tank of fuel, and the tires often won't last that long. So a race of 100 miles will require at least one pit stop. Try scheduling your races in a range of 30% to 60% of full distance.

YELLOW FLAGS

You have the option to turn off yellow flags, but that doesn't prevent wrecks. You just have to race your way through the carnage

Figure 7.6
You were pulling away from the field with 10 laps remaining when you got swept into somebody else's wreck. What do you do? Dismiss it as "just one of them racin' deals," or cheat by restarting a saved game?

of mangled machinery. Unless you're just looking to have a quick thrill with a 10-lap sprint race, don't consider this an option.

CAR DAMAGE

This isn't really an option for a race, either, except for pure arcade fun. For pre-season testing, though, you might want to turn off Car Damage while you learn the track or work on your set-up.

THE SCHEDULE

You can edit the Calendar file in the main C:\NASCAR directory to drop the tracks you really hate from the schedule. This is acceptable, but remember, you're not going to get any better at those tracks if you don't race on them. We'll look at the details of editing the season later in this chapter.

TO CHEAT OR NOT TO CHEAT

In the earlier *IndyCar Racing* simulation, Papyrus didn't include the ability to save a race in progress. They claimed a save-game option was too darned difficult to program, what with the artificial intelligence and all. But I know better. These guys insist on realism, and real racers can't stop the race because it's time for dinner. But players complained, so Papyrus gave them a save option in *NASCAR Racing*, and it makes for a quick way to cheat.

When you save a game, the race is essentially red-flagged, like race officials would do if it started raining. You restart the race under caution and get the green flag on the next lap. Depending on your track position when you stopped the race, saving can unfairly penalize you or unfairly reward you. If you were in dead last, with the leader coming up to lap you, you just got a lucky break. And you cheated. If you were in front and pulling away, stopping and saving the game will cost you that lead.

My solution: don't use the save-game feature to cheat. See "Playing by My Rules" later in this chapter.

TIP

When you're first starting out, don't make things too difficult while you learn. This game is tough enough, even after you start winning races. If you rush into your racing career running at Sears Point with opponents at 100% strength, you're in for a long and frustrating day. You have God-like power over the other drivers, so slow 'em down at first. Get comfortable at a track, both with the car set-up and your driving line, and then lower the Opponent Strength to a setting that puts you in the middle or bottom half of the pack. No sense cheating any more than you have to. As you get faster, boost your opponents' strength a bit to keep you toward the middle of the pack. With practice, you'll find yourself racing with the leaders at 100% difficulty, and sometimes even higher.

PLAYING BY MY RULES

You have lots of options, and you don't know what to do. I can help. I know, you've been anxious to read about just how I play this game.

SCHEDULE

Daytona and Indianapolis wouldn't give Papyrus the rights to include those tracks in the game. That's too bad for those tracks, and too bad for us players. I make up for the omission of Daytona by inserting a Talladega race in each of the spots on the calendar where a Daytona event would be—the season opener in February and the July 4th weekend. I figure the tracks are both about 2.5 miles, with a similar configuration. And since I can win easily at Talladega, it seems fair to me.

We'll take a closer look at editing the Calendar file later in this chapter, but here's all you do to insert Talladega into the Daytona slots. The Daytona races are listed in that file, even though they aren't in the game. Just copy the entire line of one of the Talladega races and insert that line under the Daytona entry. Unfortunately, there's no quick fix for the missing Indy speedway. If you want to run a full 32-race schedule, you can copy another event under the Indy entry.

DIVISIONS

Because of the car sets available on the on-line services, you aren't limited to the Winston Cup series. There is an excellent car set for the Busch Grand National division, which is a sort of minor league series, a step down from NASCAR's major league. The Busch races are often run as companion events to Winston Cup races, so that's how I do it. I use the same schedule as the big boys, and run a shorter Busch race before each Winston Cup race at the same track.

The Busch series runs the same car models as the Winston Cup racers, but the engines produce slightly less horsepower, so the speeds are a tick slower. To reflect this, I like to reduce Opponent Strength by 1 point for Busch races, and then limit my car's speed a bit by running a slightly taller ratio in fourth gear. We'll look at how to edit files to run multiple seasons and divisions later in this chapter.

To get a break from the grueling season—and just for fun— I run a shorter season in the International Race of Champions. This series matches drivers from different forms of racing in identically prepared stock cars. There's a good IROC car set, complete with a drivers text file, on the disk that came with this the book. More on that in Chapter 9.

RACE LENGTH

I run the Winston Cup races at 60% length. That's usually 300 miles or 300 laps, and it keeps the race time to about two hours. That leaves plenty of distance for pit stops, so you won't lose all the pit strategy that often determines the winner. The Busch races are shorter in the real world, so I set them to run at 40%.

OPPONENT STRENGTH

Start out at 100% opponent strength. If I can't begin to keep up, I'll knock down opponent strength by as much as 2 points, to 98%. I don't let myself cheat any more than that, even at those damned road courses. "Well, Ned, we'll get 'em next week."

When I can win a race with opponents at less than 100%, I bump up that rating for the next race. If I win easily at 100%— and that happens at Talladega, Michigan, Bristol, and Martinsville—I'll increase strength by 1 percentage point for the next race. If I win easily at that setting, I'll bump it up again for the next race. Don't make things too easy. Getting outrun is the surest motivation to get work harder and get faster.

SAVING

Back to that nasty cheating question again. You gotta let your conscience show you the way here. Here's what I do: save the race during every caution period. Remember to make sure all cars have finished their pit stops and you've received the One Lap to Green sign. Try never to save the game during green-flag racing.

I'm sure you're wondering: What about changing the course of history? Can I use saved games to go back in time and

Figure 7.7
Another start, another wreck. You might want to give yourself a break.

avoid that grinding crash that took me out of the race? Of course you can. It's your game. But be prepared for a late-night visit from the ghost of Fireball Roberts. "Are you sure you did the right thing, son?" he'll ask. Hey, it happened to me; I try not to cheat anymore.

The game is a little unfair to the player on starts and restarts, when you're skating around on cold tires while the computer cars look like they're riding on a rail. That makes restarts more dangerous than they should be, so give yourself a break during the first couple of laps after a restart or the start of the race. Here's my rule: if I crash on the start, I restore the race (make sure you saved after qualifying) and try again. If I wreck again on the start, I exit out to the main menu, go back to the race, skip qualifying, and start from the back of the field. Feeling pleased with myself for being so honest, I try once more. Whatever happens now, I'll take my lumps and continue the race.

Sometimes I'll cheat after an especially bizarre incident, such as getting run over while trying to make it to the pits.

If you limit your game saves to caution periods, you'll remove much of the temptation to cheat. Do you really want to go back to the last saved game after you've run green for the past hour?

TIP

Here's another reason for saving during every caution. The game doesn't have **NASCAR** caution procedures quite right. In the real world, the cars that are down a lap or more get to line up in single file to the inside of the race leaders. The game follows the simpler IndyCar rules, with the cars always restarting in single file, mixing lead-lap cars and lapped cars in the order they came out of the pits. **NASCAR** allows the leaders to bunch up for a restart, making for closer racing for position. That creates a bit of a dilemma for the ethical racing gamer, such as yourself. Saving and restarting during cautions puts all the lead-lap cars at the front of the field, with the highest-placed lapped car directly behind the last car on the lead lap. That hurts a lapped car's chances of passing the leaders and getting back on the lead lap, but it's closer to the way **NASCAR** restarts really work.

EDITING FOR FUN AND PROFIT

NASCAR Racing runs great right out of the box, but that doesn't mean you can't tinker with a few settings to make it a little better. You can change the performance of individual cars, adjust qualifying speeds, and set your own season schedule. These and other settings are in easily accessible text files that you can open and edit using Windows Notepad or another text editor.

DRIVER PERFORMANCE

Each car's performance is controlled by ratings contained in the "drivers2.txt" file, located in the appropriate Cars directory: C:\NASCAR\CARS\CARS94.

Open this file with a text editor, and then have fun changing the characteristics of these helpless drivers. Imagine if real drivers had this power: "Hmm . . . I'll just lower Dale Earnhardt's aggression rating by 200 points."

Let's look at the entry for Mark Martin:

	Traction		Aggresion
DINFO 6 1 0 475 526	**475 562**	**100 150**	**475 562**
	Power		Drag

DINFO, cleverly enough, stands for driver information. The 6 that follows is Martin's car number, the 1 tells you he drives a Ford, and the 0 means he's running Goodyear tires. If you want, you can change that information in the Driver Info section of the game, so don't worry about them here.

The next numbers are the important ones. There are four pairs of numbers, with each pair representing a value range. Reading from the left, those values represent Power, Traction, Drag, and Aggression. So Martin's Power rating ranges from 475 to 526.

TIP

You'll notice that drivers are grouped into several ranges, so that many ratings are identical. Mark Martin and Geoff Bodine, for instance, have exactly the same ratings across the board. Don't panic; that doesn't mean that those two cars will run identical speeds at every track. Remember, a game chooses a random number from within those ranges for every race, so they're never going to be exactly the same at any given race.

The Power rating dictates acceleration; Traction governs cornering speed; Aggression indicates how easily the driver will move over when challenged; and Drag dictates wind resistance and straightaway speed.

The base line for these ratings is 500, and that value is adjusted up and down to reflect relative ratings for each driver. A good driver, using the Ace set-up, should be roughly even with a computer-controlled car running with 500s across the board, set to 100% strength.

For Power, Traction, and Aggression, a higher number indicates higher performance. For Drag, a lower number means less wind resistance and faster speeds.

The game randomly selects a number within each range, generating a different number for each session: Practice, Qualifying, and Race. The wider the range, the less consistent that car will be. The system works very well, so you might find Martin dominating one week and barely able to crack the top-20 in the next race. Sorta like life.

WARNING Always edit the "drivers2.txt" file. The "drivers.txt" file, found in the same directory, serves as a back-up file. If you get things screwed up by changing the "drivers2.txt" file, restore the original values by deleting the "drivers2.txt" file and renaming "drivers.txt" to "drivers2.txt." Try again, but remember: the original values make for close, balanced racing, so don't go overboard when you're changing them.

TWEAKING THE TRACKS

There are a few adjustments you can make safely in the track text files, but be very careful changing these numbers. You can really screw up the game balance, so let's limit editing options here.

Figure 7.8
You can't change the track, but you can change the way computer cars run there.

You'll find the track text files in the respective track subdirectories. The "atlanta.txt" file is located at C:\NASCAR\ TRACKS\ATLANTA. Unlike the "drivers2.txt" file, there is no backup file, so back up the original file before you start hacking.

ADJUSTING QUALIFYING SPEEDS

Slow qualifying speeds for the player are a chronic problem in *NASCAR Racing*. Even with a fast qualifying set-up, your relative speeds in practice and during the race are much faster than in qualifying. That's a distinct disadvantage, since you're going to be slower than the computer cars for the first couple of laps after the green flag.

There are a couple of ways to remedy this. One is to adjust the Opponent Strength in the game Options menu, setting it 1 or 2 points lower for qualifying, and then bumping it back up for the race. That's a little awkward, though, since you have to save the race weekend and exit to the main menu to change the strength, and then restart the race.

You can get the same results by changing the BLAP value in the "track.txt" file, so you don't have to go back and forth to readjust the race speed from inside the game. The BLAP number dictates qualifying speed for computer cars. In the "atlanta.txt" file, for example, that number is 31583. That figure is actually a lap time, and should be read 31.583 seconds. To slow down qualifying speeds, increase the number slightly. Don't deal in seconds, or you'll slow speeds drastically. Adjust this number in tenths of a second, or even hundredths, if your handicap is slight.

Trial and error is the only way to get an accurate adjustment. Determine how fast you're running in the Pre-Race Practice, and where your speed places you among your competitors. Then check your speed in qualifying trim, and see how it stacks up against the rest of the cars. Adjust the BLAP number upward to slow down the other cars and bring the relative practice and qualifying speeds into line. If you're running fifth-fastest in practice, slow down the field so that your qualifying speed puts you about fifth. This will take a while, and the adjustment will be different for each track.

RACE ADJUSTMENTS

You can also adjust the relative strength of the computer cars at each track, but you should consider this a last resort. Find the RELS value in the "track.txt," on the line directly below BLAP in the "track.txt" file. This value is a 100-base number, and is separate from the percentage you set in the game under Opponent Strength. Adjusting the RELS value has the same effect, but a change here has no effect on the Opponent Strength number in the game. The advantage in changing the "track.txt" file is that you don't have to change the Opponent Strength from Game Options when you go from track to track.

In the "atlanta.txt" file, the RELS number is 98. Adjust this number up or down to change the speed of the entire field, except for your car. Again, do this only where there's a major discrepancy in your speed relative to the computer cars. If you're consistently outrunning the competition badly at, say, Michigan, then increase that track's RELS value by 1.

You should probably limit RELS changes to tracks where you're significantly faster than your computer opponents. The computer cars won't get faster on their own, but *you* can. If you

Figure 7.9
Things get mighty
crowded at
Martinsville
with 40 cars
on the track.

slow down the field permanently by adjusting RELS, you'll have less incentive to learn to get around that track faster. Resort to slowing the field only at tracks where you're convinced you'll never get much faster. The road courses, maybe?

With lots of trial and error, you can adjust the BLAP and RELS values so that you never have to touch Opponent Strength number from within the game. Each track will be tweaked for close competition and fair qualifying speeds.

FIELD SIZE

The number of cars that start a race varies from track to track, from 39 at the larger speedways down to 28 to 33 at the smaller tracks. That's the way NASCAR does it, but it's not quite fair in the game. The cars that will participate in a race are determined solely by their order in the game, as shown in the Drive Info section of the game. If you're running 38 opponents, the last few cars in that listing will never get to start races on the short tracks.

If this bit of injustice keeps you awake at night, you can adjust the field size for the shorter tracks to include everybody. In the "track.txt" file, find the CARS entry with two numbers beside it. At Martinsville, for example, those numbers are 33 33. Change that number to 40 40 to set the field to the maximum size. Watch out, though: that's a lot of cars for a half-mile race track. It's not exactly realistic, but those forgotten drivers at the end of the line will thank you. Of course, one of them might put you into the wall, too.

SETTING YOUR OWN SCHEDULE

The season schedule is yours to modify just about any way you like. Find the "calendar" file (there is no extension) in the main C:\NASCAR directory. Open it with a text editor and let's take a look.

Ignore the entries for Daytona and Indianapolis. They're in this file, but they won't show up in the game. If you have the Track Pack, the first entry after Daytona is Atlanta. With the Track Pack, you start out at Rockingham.

CHANGING THE DATE

Looking at the Atlanta entry, the first two sets of numbers are simply the date of that race—3 13 means March 13. The third number indicates if that race is the first or second at the track for the season: 0 is the first race at that track; 1 is the second race of the season there. Don't worry about this number.

NIGHT AND DAY

The next number is either 0 or 1, and determines whether the race is held during the day or at night: 0 for day and 1 for night. In real life, the only night races are held at Charlotte, Bristol, and Richmond—one event at each track, for three night races during the season. It's your game, so you can run every race at night if you want, just by changing that 0 to 1. The other tracks aren't equipped with lights, of course, but there must be a full moon.

EDITING THE SCHEDULE

The stock "calendar" is accurate for the 1994 schedule, but that doesn't mean you can't change it. You can delete tracks or schedule more or fewer races at them.

If you don't like a certain track—or you're just getting tired of having your doors blown off there—you can just delete that entry from the "calendar" file. Junior Johnson would probably sneer at you if he knew, but chances are he'll never find out.

You can alter the order of races simply by moving the entries around. You'll want to change the dates, of course, at least if you have any allegiance to the linear progression of time. To make up for the absence of Daytona and Indianapolis and to run a full 32-race schedule, see "Playing by My Rules" earlier in this chapter.

RUNNING MULTIPLE SEASONS

NASCAR Racing doesn't have a built-in feature to allow you to run different seasons, with different car sets, at the same time. With a little file editing, however, you can do this for yourself pretty easily.

You need to manipulate two files: "calendar" and "season.bin," both in the main C:\NASCAR directory. Let's say you want to run simultaneous seasons for Winston Cup, Busch Grand National, and the International Race of Champions. Start with the "calendar" file, and set up a 32-race schedule. Save two copies of that file under different names, one called "calendar.wc" and another named "calendar.bgn." Now edit the "calendar" file another time to create a shorter schedule—eight races, maybe—for an IROC series. Save that file as "calendar.irc." Don't worry about the "season.bin" file for now.

Let's say you want to run a Busch race first. Rename "calendar.bgn" to "calendar" (you may have to delete the original "calendar" file first). Run the race—saving as you normally would, if necessary—and then exit the game. Rename "calendar" to "calendar.bgn," and rename "season.bin" to "season.bgn."

Now you're ready to run a Winston Cup race. Rename "calendar.wc" to "calendar," and start the season. After you finish the first race, rename "calendar" to "calendar.wc" and "season.bin" to "season.wc." Repeat the process to start your IROC season.

Figure 7.10
There it is. Your own paint shop, where you can turn your sick mind loose to design your own cars.

It takes a bit of file management, but this system will let you run different series, complete with their own schedules and points standings.

TIP You must have a "calendar" file to start or resume a season. The game will create a "season.bin" file when you start a new season, so you don't have to worry about saving "season.bin" under another name until you've started a season.

FUN WITH PAINT KIT

You've chosen your car, assembled a top-notch crew, sharpened your driving skills, and put in countless hours in the garage and on the track working on set-ups. It's about time you landed yourself a sponsor to bankroll your drive for the championship.

That's where the Paint Kit comes in. It's a simple program, but Paint Kit opens up a world of possibilities in your career as team owner and racing commissioner. You decide who races, you design your own car. This is, after all, your game.

PAINT YOUR WAGON

The possibilities are limited only by your imagination—and by your skill as a graphics artist. How about a car bearing the logo of your company, or your college or high school alma mater? Favorite rock band? Or how about a car dedicated to your mother? Just about anything's possible, so get out the spray cans and brushes and get started. You don't even have to worry about cleaning up when you're done.

The Papyrus manual covers this subject thoroughly, so I won't waste your time with the details of painting and pasting decals. Instead, lets look at some ways to make the Paint Kit easier to use, and some tips to get the best results.

WARNING Don't edit the "cars94.dat" file. Create another subdirectory under C:\NASCAR called "cars95," along with another data file, "cars95.dat." The program will do this for you. Start Paint Kit by typing "paintkit cars95" at the command prompt. The program will ask you if you want to create that directory and that data file. Answer "yes" to both questions, and you'll have a duplicate car set to splatter with paint. Whatever you do, don't delete or rename C:\NASCAR\CARS \CARS94, even if you never use that car set. *NASCAR Racing* won't run without those file and path names; change anything here and you'll have to reinstall the whole game.

MAKING TEMPLATES

To save yourself time, make a template of each car model: Ford Thunderbird, Chevy Lumina, Pontiac Gran Prix, and maybe the new Chevy Monte Carlo, if you have one. From the Cars94 set, find a car to represent each model, and then paint it solid white, remove all the decals, and save the file, calling it "chevy.pcx" and so on. Store these template files in a separate subdirectory. Then, when you're ready to create the new crop of cars for the 1996 season, you'll have a clean slate to work with.

GO WILD, YOUNG MAN

Wanna go up against Earnhardt and Gordon in your hot-rod Honda Civic, or a Dodge Ram pick-up truck? You can, if you hold a steady mouse and have a fine eye for detail. You can paint new grills, bumpers, windows, and trim to create all sorts of vehicles. Your most serious limitation is in the shape of your dream ride. It's gonna be square, so don't bother trying to design a Volkswagen Beetle.

Other than that limitation, the sky's the limit. Some of the more ambitious artists out there have come up with nice-looking Camaros, Trans-Ams, a Porsche 911, a Ford Taurus, and even a pick-up.

I'm no artist, so I'd rather climb into the fine cars created by others and uploaded to on-line services. I'm a driver, dammit, not a graphics artist!

Chris Frederick, Dave Upson, Manuel Daskolos, and others have come up with some gems, and they're yours for the taking. Just be sure to thank 'em. More on custom car-sets in Chapter 9.

TIP   There's no way to change car sets from within the Paint Kit program. You must specify the car set when you start the program. At the DOS prompt, in the main NASCAR directory, type "paintkit cars94" to open the graphics from the Cars94 set. To open a different set, change "cars94" to the one you want. If you don't specify a car set, Paint Kit automatically opens Cars94.

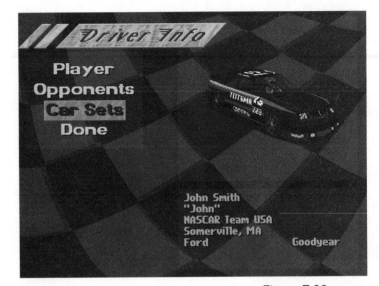

Figure 7.11
Prefer something sportier?
Check out this
Camaro Z-28.

USING OTHER PAINT PROGRAMS

Although it gives you the ability to create your own cars and paint schemes, Paint Kit is a fairly simple graphics tool. If you're familiar with other paint programs—or you're just adventurous—you can try your hand with one of the more sophisticated programs.

THE BASICS

NASCAR Racing and the Paint Kit program use the PCX file format. Various commercial paint programs allow you to edit those files, just as you do in Paint Kit. In general, the paint programs give you more more tools than you'll find in Paint Kit. NeoPaint is a popular shareware program, and it's for download on the major on-line services.

Using a paint program such as NeoPaint allows you to convert graphics from other formats, including scanned images, resize them and use them in Paint Kit. You can also create decal graphics that can be imported into Paint Kit.

HOW TO DO IT

Use the pace car from the Cars94 car set, or a car template used for painting cars. In Paint Kit, export the graphic. The file should be in the C:\NASCAR directory with a PCX extension. From NeoPaint or another paint program, open the file and get creative. You can paint the car, insert text in different fonts, and even cut and paste images from other graphics.

Be warned, though, that Paint Kit uses a lower resolution, so any high-res work you do in another program will be lost when you import a graphic into Paint Kit. If the image is too complex, it just won't show up in Paint Kit or in the game. Try to limit your work to just a few colors, and keep it simple.

WARNING Some of the more sophisticated paint programs, such as CorelDraw, won't work with Paint Kit files. These programs have a much larger color palette than Paint Kit, and that palette will be lost when you try to import the graphic into Paint Kit.

IMPORTING CAR GRAPHICS

Hats off to Papyrus for giving us a way to design cars and import them into the game. It would have been nice, though, if it weren't such a clumsy process. But while it may be a bit akward to import a custom car, there are just a few steps to follow. You'll need a minimal knowledge of the file structure on your computer, and how to get at those files. We'll assume you're using File Manager in Windows or Windows 95.

CHANGING YOUR CAR

Here are step-by-step instructions for changing the player's car graphic. The example assumes you're replacing your car with a custom car that you've downloaded from an on-line service.

- Start NASCAR Paint Kit and select Paint Car.
- Scroll to the car you want to change (NASCAR #94).
- Click the Export button on the bottom menu.
- Exit Paint Kit.
- Enter Windows File Manager.
- Create a subdirectory under C:\NASCAR\CARS called ORIGINAL.
- Find the "nasc94.pcx" file in the C:\NASCAR directory. This is the car graphic you exported from Paint Kit.
- Move "nasc94.pcx" into C:\NASCAR\CARS\ORIGINAL (in case you want to use that car graphic again).
- Find the file for the car graphic you want to use, and then rename it to "naxc94.pcx." Copy or move that file into the C:\NASCAR directory.
- Start Paint Kit, enter the Paint Shop, and find the original car you want to replace.
- Click on Import on the menu. You should be looking at the paint scheme of your new car.
- Go to Paint Suit to match your team color to your new car's paint scheme.
- Click Save.

It's not nearly as complicated as it sounds. Just remember that the program requires that new file to have the same name as the old one. The graphic for the first car in line—yours—will always be called "nasc94.pcx", whether you're running the original # 94 car or a #686 hot rod of your own design.

THE MOST
DANGEROUS DRIVER

Games People Play

YOU'VE **FINE-TUNED YOUR CAR AND YOUR DRIVING SKILLS** until you're almost unbeatable. You're trouncing Jeff Gordon, Mark Martin, and the rest of NASCAR's elite just about every time out. Well, at least you're outrunning their cars. In reality, of course, you're racing against nothing but a set of instructions written by a computer programmer. Sure, it's exciting enough, and you swear sometimes the guy behind you gets angry when you won't get out of his way. But it's just not the same as racing against a real person, somebody who might be as good—and unpredictable—as you.

There are two ways to play against a real live human, and either one is a big improvement over racing against the computer-controlled cars. You can hook up directly with a partner via a modem, or you can test your skills against a full field of other gamers on The Papyrus Network, a multi-player service. Either way, you're in for a thrill you simply won't find racing against computer-controlled cars.

MODEM MATCH-UPS

With a modem and a racing partner, you're in business. You've blown the doors off the computer cars; now let's see how you stack up against your buddy across town.

WHAT YOU NEED

To connect via modem for some two-player racing, all you need is a 9600-baud modem or faster and a willing partner. Consult the manual for instructions on modem settings.

FIND AN OPPONENT

So you're itching to race a live person, but you don't know anyone in town. The on-line services can help. America Online,

CompuServe, and Prodigy all have forums devoted to modem racing. That's where you'll find other racers hungry for some action.

Post an invitation that lists your area code and you just might find somebody nearby who's willing to race. If you're lucky, it'll be somebody that's only a local phone call away.

HOOKING UP

You'll save yourself—and the person on the other end of the line—a lot of frustration if you spend a little time in preparation before you try to connect. Make sure you know the model name of your modem, which COM port it uses, and its baud rate.

If you find your modem listed in the Specify Modem section under Multiplayer, then you're in business. Just pick your brand and you should be ready to race. Otherwise, dig out your modem manual from the bottom of the drawer and find the proper initialization string. Enter this in the Custom Setup section of Multiplayer.

OPTIONS

OK, so I'm a stickler for realism. It might be fun to run a demolition derby every now and then, with Car Damage turned off so that you can run wild and wreck the rest of the field. But this is a simulation, and you'll get more out of it if you play it straight. You may want to run shorter races—especially if you're dialing long-distance—but try to run at least 100 miles, so that you'll have to play some pit strategy. While you're at it, leave the Pace Lap and Yellow Flag options on.

You have to make the same choices for modem racing, but remember: gear the settings for the slower computer. If your buddy's running a Pentium 60 and you're screaming on a 133 MHz machine, running against a full field of 38 computer cars might not be fair to the other guy. After all, you want to be fair when you blow his doors off and send him home crying to his mommy.

Figure 8.1
If that's your modem buddy that you just spun out, get ready for some revenge.

USE THE SAME CAR GRAPHICS

Each player will see the race through the eyes of his computer, using his own car-set. If you're using different car-sets, the players will be in different cars, at least as it appears to the other player. Sort of a Star Trek parallel universe thing. While you see the other guy driving Jeff Gordon's # 24, he thinks he's driving the NASCAR #50. That's weird, so you should fix it by using the same set of car graphics and "drivers2.txt" files on both computers.

SET THE RULES FIRST

Don't touch that dial—at least until you and your racing partner decide on options. Number of computer cars, damage, yellow flags, pace lap, length of race, weather—none of these variables can be changed once you link up for some modem racing. If you decide to change any of those options, you'll have to hang up and call again.

The person who receives the phone call is the one whose settings are in effect. Get everything set before the scheduled modem hook-up.

RUNNING A SEASON

There's no championship season available in modem play, but that doesn't mean you can't create one. You'll have to keep track of the standings yourself, assigning points based on the finishing order of each race.

Decide on a season schedule, and then agree on the start time for each race, along with other options. If you know how to use a spreadsheet, you can set up one to keep track of the points standings, wins, and so on.

TIP So you want to run a full 500-mile race against your cocky friend across town? You're free to do it, but be ready for a long drive. There's no way to Pause or Save the game when you're hooked up live. After three or four hours of heart-pounding racing, they may have to help you out of your chair to administer oxygen and treat you for heat exhaustion.

CHATTING

The primary function of Chat Mode is, of course, to taunt your opponent. Besides ridicule, you can use Chat to let both players agree to begin different sessions of the Race Weekend. The answering computer is in charge, so it's up to that player to begin sessions. Just make sure your partner is ready before you decide to start the race.

STRATEGIES

It's tempting to go nuts when you're racing against a real, live human being for the first time. You'll want to wreck each other, drive the wrong way around the track, and generally act like a couple of fools as you rejoice in the wonders of modem racing. When you get over that initial madness, though, you'll want to do some real racing. Here are a few things to keep in mind.

USING COMPUTER CARS

You might want to get your modem "legs" by running a bit of mano-o-mano racing, but eventually you'll want to run with some computer-controlled cars on the track. It's more fun, and it's a stiffer challenge, as you and your buddy battle traffic. You might be racing the other guy for the lead, or you might be fighting for 20th place. That's two races in one: trying to outrun your modem partner while you fight against the computer cars.

DON'T RACE EACH OTHER

Naturally, you'll want to keep an eye on your modem partner as you work your way through traffic. That's why you're doing this, after all. But don't get so focused on the other guy that you forget about the computer cars. Run the race as you normally do, trying to outrun both your modem opponent and the computer-controlled cars.

Unless the two modem opponents are pretty close in driving skills, they may not run together very much on the track. That's OK; the slower guy will just have to get better. Believe me, getting outrun badly by a smart-aleck acquaintance is the best motivation to get faster.

TIP

If you're a veteran racer running against a rookie, you can use modem racing to help bring your buddy up to speed. Set the Number of Opponents to one, so it'll be just the two of you. Set Car Damage off, and use the same car set-up. Using Chat Mode, give your rookie partner tips on getting around the track. Let him follow you around for a lap or two at reduced speed to get a feel for the driving line. When you bring your partner up to speed, it's time to go racing.

Figure 8.2
This is an early, rough draft of The Papyrus Network intro screen. You can outrun the computer; now get ready for the real thing.

YOU'VE GOT A FRIEND

While you shouldn't focus solely on your human opponent if you're also running against computer cars, you can team up with the other guy to the benefit of both. Pretend you two are part of a two-car race team. You're both trying to win, but you can play a team strategy to help each car outrun computer cars.

At the tracks where the draft plays a key role—mainly Talladega and Pocono—modem players can draft together to help catch the lead pack. If you lose the draft at Talladega, you're out of luck until you catch a caution flag or the leaders run into slower traffic. With a partner, though, you can stay in a two-car draft and pick up 2 or 3 mph. Before the race, practice drafting with your partner, running in tight formation, as close together as possible. Try switching the order to see which car pulls the two-car draft faster. On race day, you might be able to stick together and blow away the rest of the field. When it comes down to the end, though, that partnership disappears as you battle with your buddy for the win.

THE PAPYRUS NETWORK

Running against another human driver is a cool change of pace from racing solo against the computer. But what would it be like to run against 20 or 30 other guys? With The Papyrus Network, a multi-player racing network, you can find out. You'll also find out just how good you are, as you match your set-ups and driving skills against racers from all over the country.

WHAT IT IS

As I write this, the Network is still under construction, so the details aren't set. But one thing's for sure: it's a blast. Computer racers dial in to "server" computers run by Papyrus. Once you get there, you can swap some tall tales with fellow drivers, and then pick a race that suits you and go swap paint with a full field of real drivers.

There'll be season championships, various divisions, and plenty of choices for race length and driving skill. Whether you're a local champ or a beginner, you'll find competition to match your ability.

It's still in the planning stages, so don't hold Papyrus to it. But they're trying to get a few real NASCAR drivers to join in the fun (and the mayhem). How'd you like to run at Charlotte against the defending World 600 champ, Bobby Labonte? Stay tuned. It just might happen.

Of course, you'll have to set up an account and pay for the service. Papyrus wants you to have fun, but it ain't free. The price structure of the service hadn't been set by the time this book was published.

WHAT YOU NEED

The multi-player service requires a separate program from the one that came on the *NASCAR Racing* CD or disks when you bought the game. Contact Papyrus to find out how to get the network version of the game. It will be a free upgrade. The multi-player program will have all the other information you need, including the telephone number to dial in your area.

Other than a modem and nerves of steel, that's all you need to go network racing. Get ready for the thrill of a lifetime.

HOW IT WORKS

Again, I'm basing these descriptions on my experiences during the test program for The Papyrus Network. The service you find will be different—and better—after Papyrus fine-tunes the Network and adds features.

After you set up an account and log in to the service, you'll see a menu that lets you access your mail box to check on late-breaking Network news, as well as chat with other drivers. But since you're ready for some action, you'll want to go to the scheduling area right away.

Some players, along with the Papyrus people, will act as commissioners, setting the rules and scheduling races. A menu will show you the races that are forming, along with race length and other options. Find a track you like, and you're a keystroke away from a whole new world of racing.

Once you choose a race, you'll be back on familiar turf. The multi-player racing program will start, and you'll go directly to the race menu. Load your best set-up and get out there for the practice session. The race administrator will let you know when practice is over. You'll move on to qualifying and then the race.

STRATEGIES

Forget everything I've told you about strategies to outrun and outwit the computer drivers. Running against real people is a whole new game. Some of these drivers are aces, some are good, and some should probably stick to playing *Doom*. There'll be some sort of tiering system to pit drivers of similar skills against each other. Even so, always keep in mind that these aren't mindless computer instructions you're racing against. These drivers might be just as wild and unpredictable as you are.

QUALIFYING

The simple step of qualifying is an important one to take against computer-controlled drivers. Against real racers, it can be critical. There will likely be lots of crashes, and you may be running with no yellow flags. Starting near the front can keep a lot of that trouble behind you and let you concentrate on racing.

SURVIVE THE START

That start of a race is always a dangerous moment, but with 20 hot-headed, lead-footed drivers—all on cold tires—the drop of the green flag in a Network race often signals the start of a demolition derby.

Don't try to win the race on the first lap. Unless you're starting on the front row, fall in line and just try to hold your line without crunching into another car. Watch for trouble in front, and keep tabs on the position of the car behind you. After the field gets sorted out a lap or two into the race, you can settle in and look to make your move.

TAKE IT EASY

If you're racing against rookies—or you're a rookie yourself— you'll fare better in Network racing by playing it safe. "Race the track," as they say, instead of looking to outrun every car that gets near you. You shouldn't ignore the other cars, of course, and you'll get plenty of chances to show your brilliant passing maneuvers after you get more comfortable on the track. But if you're just starting out, try to run consistent laps and hold your line while all the high-speed madness breaks out around you. If you can finish the race, chances are you'll finish high in the final standings.

MAKE SOME FRIENDS

When you're running Talladega, try to find a drafting partner before you go to the track. If you can make a friend and stick to him during the race, the two of you—or more—can use the draft to work your way through the field and to the front. If the race is long enough to require pit stops, work those out in advance, too, so that your group can pit at the same time and maintain the draft when you go back out onto the track.

A NIGHT AT THE RACES

Yeah, I was kickin' butt and taking names. Two-time NASCAR champion, 27 wins, and millions in winnings. My two cross-town modem buddies were good, but no real match for me. That's right, I was the next Richard Petty. And then I went racing on The Papyrus Network.

Here's an account of my first night of Network racing. *Warning:* some of the descriptions here are intended for mature audiences. Some language may not be suitable for children under 17.

HOOKING UP

I've thought about little else all day, and work has just gotten in the way. Tonight I'm going racing on the Network. I order pasta for lunch to keep me sharp—an athlete's meal. Well, a pizza buffet, really; but close enough.

I spend the early evening fine-tuning set-ups and getting in some practice at a few tracks. I don't know where they're running tonight, but I figure Talladega's a good bet, along with Michigan, since they're both pretty easy tracks. And that's just the problem, although I don't know the extent of my handicap yet. I win easily against the computer cars at those tracks, so I haven't put a lot of effort into getting quicker there. That laziness will soon cost me.

HANDSHAKES ALL AROUND

The Network opens at 9:00 p.m. At about 8:00, I dial up the Papyrus bulletin board to download the multi-player program, "multi.exe." Back home and off line, I run the program to set up my modem and graphics preferences.

Promptly at 9:00, I dial the Network and log in as one of the beta testers. After poking around a bit—no mail is waiting—and saying hello to the Papyrus guys, I go to the scheduler to see what's happening. A dozen other drivers are already there, greeting one another and swapping racing stories.

Two races have been nominated, a 15-lapper at Atlanta and a longer run at Sears Point. The veteran Network drivers are going to Sears Point for a series points race, so that's not for me. These are the top drivers, and I'm new to multi-player racing. No sense in screwing up the race for those guys. So it's Atlanta. The race administrator has set an eight-car minimum for the race, and it takes a few minutes for enough drivers to join. When the eighth driver jumps in, I go directly to the track menu.

BURNING AT ATLANTA

Here we go. Fifteen laps, car damage on, no yellow flags, with a pace lap. After I load my best Atlanta race set-up, I reduce the fuel load to 8 gallons, plenty enough to go the distance. I also shorten the fourth-gear ratio one step, figuring that I can turn the motor a little tighter for such a short race. Than it's out onto the track for practice.

Coming out of the pits, I stay low on the apron of the track through turns 1 and 2. There are already some cars on the track running at full speed, so I don't want to get in their way. When the traffic clears, I stand on the gas and get ready to turn some hot laps. After a few turns around Atlanta, I'm running consistent laps at 177–178 mph. That's good enough to run up front at my house, but against these guys that puts me in the middle of the pack.

I'm still on the track when the practice session ends and we go to qualifying. I load my qualifying set-up and head out onto the track. There's no waiting in line; everybody can run at the same time, with no one else on the track. I take the green flag, and then the car jumps out from underneath me coming off of turn 2. I save it, but that slip screwed up my lap. The speed: 176.311, good for seventh starting position in the 12-car line-up. That's well off my practice speeds, and much slower than the pole speed of 183 + mph.

After qualifying is complete, I go back to the garage and raise the rear spoiler by 2 degrees. It's a gamble, but I'm getting outrun through the corners. I'll sacrifice a bit of straightaway speed to get through the turns faster.

It's race time. The field forms behind the pace car to take a pace lap before getting the green flag. My seventh starting spot puts me on the inside of row 4. I plan to hold my line and take the bottom groove through turn 1. Coming off of turn 4, the green flag waves and the 12 cars roar to life, accelerating down the front stretch.

Cars are scrambling for position all around me, and suddenly two cars bang together up ahead and go sliding out of control. The car directly in front of me gets swept up into the wall, but I manage to drive right through the middle of the carnage. There are no caution flags in this race, so I stay on the throttle as I maneuver through the debris.

When the smoke clears, I'm running second, about 2 seconds behind the leader and 1.5 seconds ahead of third place. Four cars, mangled in the wreck, are forced to pit. I watch the chat line on my screen, and enjoy seeing the accusations fly as the drivers of the wrecked cars calmly discuss the incident.

With no others cars immediately around me, I settle in and start clicking off some pretty quick laps: consistent 178s, and then a couple at more than 179 mph. It's not enough. The leader, the guy who won the pole, is slowly pulling away. My only hope is to stay as close as possible and hope he gets caught in some slower traffic.

The battle for second is a good one. The guy behind me gains a couple of tenths on one lap, and I regain the advantage on the next one. There are only four laps left; I can hold him off. But I've driven the car too hard through the corners, abusing that right-front tire. The car has developed a push through the turns, and it gets progressively worse. With two laps to go, I slap the outside wall coming out of turn 4. My car spins to the inside down the front straightaway, but I manage to avoid the inside wall. The right-front fender is crumpled, so I pull back onto the inside of the track and limp toward the checkered flag. I finish 11th out of 12 drivers. And I'm pissed.

RUNNIN' THE ROCK

After watching some replays of my Atlanta wreck, I return to the scheduler and find two races nominated: Rockingham and Pocono. The Rock's tough, but I haven't run Pocono lately, so I go to the 1-mile oval at Rockingham.

Figure 8.3
Yeah, that's my
#16 sliding out of
control toward
destruction at
Talladega. "We
had 'em covered,
Ned. I was just
bidin' my time
when some idiot
ran all over me."

Fifteen cars this time, no cautions, car damage on, 25 laps. I qualify 10th, but there's another melee early in the race that takes out a few faster cars. I avoid trouble, turn some quick laps, and pull off a nice pass toward the end to finish third, within sight of the leaders. Not bad.

TANGLE AT TALLADEGA

When I return from The Rock, there's a race forming at Talladega, so I jump right in. In practice, my laps in the 193.5 range are about a half-mile-an-hour slower than the fastest cars. If I can hang on to the lead draft, though, I might be able to finish up front.

I qualify at 193.226 mph, putting me eighth among the 13 cars. The start of the race is bedlam, but it's clean this time. Everybody makes it through the first turns in good shape, and we settle in for some drafting fun. I'm running seventh, with the eighth-place car close behind, when a group of cars gets out of shape coming through the tri-oval. They don't crash, but they slow down just enough to let me sail by without cracking the throttle. I'm fourth now, and I can see the lead trio, running about a second ahead of me.

My nemesis is still on my tail, but our draft is now catching the third-place car, which has fallen back a bit from the two leaders. With six laps to go, we probably can't catch the front two cars, but we're closing fast on third. As we come off turn 4, the fourth-place guy dives to the inside. Now there are plenty of good places to pass at Talladega, but the tri-oval dogleg isn't one of them. It's tough enough to make it through there at full speed by yourself. Going through there side-by-side with another car is just begging for a crash.

I have a choice: do I back off and let him go, or do I keep it to the floor and hope for the best? Hell no, I don't back off. I didn't make the dumb move. So I keep the pedal floored and cut the dogleg with the other car to my inside. Sure enough, we get together and slide off through the grass. I hit the inside wall at about 180 mph and my pretty car explodes into a shower of debris. My unwise opponent does the same.

Our cars come to rest just a few feet apart, so close that I can see him behind the wheel of his crashed race car. I hit F10 and type "What the *@*&)*! are you doing passing in the dogleg?" "My mistake," he answers. Oh well, just one of them racin' deals.

HUMBLED AT CHARLOTTE

Charlotte's next up. The double-dogleg on the front stretch makes this a tough track, yet I'm usually able to outrun the computer cars here. But tonight I'm in for a lesson on getting around this 1.5-mile track.

I qualify near the rear of the 12-car field, and I'm never a real factor. I work my way up to eighth when I smack the wall coming out of turn 4. With the right-front destroyed, my car slides back across the track, collecting two cars running behind me. We're all out of the race. "Sorry, guys. My fault," I type. I'll have to put in some practice and garage time before I return to Charlotte.

MARTINSVILLE MADNESS

With a badly bruised ego, I return to the scheduler and get ready to take my lumps from the guys I wrecked. They take it easy on me, though. They're disappointed, though they understand that mistakes happen.

It's getting late, and I haven't run a short-track race yet, so I nominate Martinsville: 50 laps, car damage on, pace lap on, no yellows. Other guys jump in and we quickly have a 14-car field.

In the garage, I load my trusty Martinsville set-up and reduce the fuel load to run 50 laps. I'm second-fastest in practice, topping out at 96.239 mph. As usual, I'm slower in qualifying, managing only 94.521, good enough for the third starting spot.

We take the green flag, and it quickly becomes apparent that some of these guys are too aggressive on this tight track. Cars slam together in front of and behind me, but I steer clear of the wreckage and emerge in fourth.

There are eight of us left, all pretty close together. The fourth-place car slips in turns 1 and 2, and I drive past and take the spot. The race remains stable for the next 30 laps, and I'm turning consistent laps at 95 mph. The lead car has pulled away to a 5-second lead, and he looks untouchable. I'm maintaining a 2-second lead over fourth place, and I'm gaining slowly on the second-place car.

With five laps to go, I'm on his bumper. I follow in his tire tracks, cooling my tires and waiting for him to make a mistake. He doesn't slip, holding the low groove through the corners and keeping me at bay. We take the white flag and I make my move, driving into turn 1 harder than I have all race. He's a few feet from the bottom of the track, leaving just enough room to get my car's bumper up alongside him on the inside. I pull even.

We race side-by-side down the back stretch, but I've got a firm claim to the inside lane. I hold my line, riding him up on the track as we hit turn 3. Our cars touch, and both of us fight for control. We cross the finish line sideways, door handle to door handle. And he beats me by a foot to take second.

"Good race," he tells me. "That was great," I reply, with amazing calm. "Let's do it again."

LESSONS LEARNED

As I try to get to sleep that night, I review the evening's races. I screwed up at Atlanta, survived at Rockingham, got wrecked at Talladega, and ran near the front at Martinsville. A thrilling night of racing, but I want more. I'll go back to the garage tomorrow, to see if I can squeeze a bit more speed out of my set-ups. I'm going to need it, because I won't be happy 'til I win.

If you like *NASCAR Racing,* then you're going to go crazy over The Papyrus Network. I guarantee it. Gotta go now, I need to find 1 more mile an hour in my 'Dega set-up. Maybe I'll see *you* there next time.

CYBER-
RACING

The On-Line Racing Community

One of the surest ways to find the quality games is to check out the on-line forums. The games that are creating the most conversation are probably the best titles available. That's true of *NASCAR Racing*, which has generated an avalanche of material on the major on-line services since its release.

And there's more than just idle chatter. The people who love this game are also working hard to make it even better. There are hundreds of files available for download that will make *NASCAR Racing* easier and more enjoyable. And the forums are such a good place to make new friends. Your mother will be pleased.

FILES TO DOWNLOAD

There's a wealth of excellent graphics, programs, and help files available on the Internet and the commercial on-line services. I've hunted down the best of these little gems, including complete car-sets, some cool car designs, lightning-fast car set-ups, and several editing programs to help you get more out of *NASCAR Racing*.

All programs and files described were uploaded to on-line services as freeware, so they're readily available for your own use or for distribution. I've tested them all and haven't found any problems, but neither I, nor Sybex, nor Papyrus can guarantee them. Use them at your own risk (and always check for viruses). And, please, don't call us with questions about these files.

I've tried to credit the authors and artists who created these utilities and graphics, but some of you people didn't identify yourselves. Thanks to all of you who've made this great game more enjoyable for us all.

WHERE TO FIND IT

You can find most of these files and programs in the Motorsports library in the Sports Simulations forum on

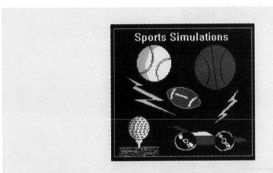

Sports Simulations Forum

CompuServe, but there are a lot of other non-NASCAR files there, too. For the sake of convenience, I've taken the best stuff and put it on a CD-ROM Disk.

CAR-SETS AND GRAPHICS

Disappointed that Dale Earnhardt wasn't in the car included with the game? Ol' Ironhead didn't give Papyrus the rights to use his car or name, but that legal obstacle doesn't stop the players themselves from creating that dreaded black #3. In the third-party NASCAR car-sets that *are* available on-line, you'll find Earnhardt and many other drivers and cars not included with the game.

Winston Cup isn't the only game in town, so I've included some of the better alternative car-sets so that you can run different racing series.

There's also some fun stuff here, including some street cars and some pretty wild designs. You might find some to your liking, or you might be inspired to create your own.

1995 WINSTON CUP CAR-SET   CARS95CF

There are several current car-sets floating around cyberspace, but this one from Chris Frederick is my favorite. You get

Figure 9.2
Sorry, Papyrus, but some of the car-sets available on-line look even better than the originals.

first-rate graphics and a drivers file that results in competitive and realistic racing. This file is updated throughout the season, with performance based on the points standings, so check in CompuServe's Motorsports library to get the most recent version. This one is a must for any serious fan of *NASCAR Racing*.

TEAM USA MONTE CARLO   MCRL094

If you feel left out because you're stuck with a Lumina while the real racers are tearing up the circuit in the new Monte Carlo, then this car's for you. It's the same basic design as the player's #F94 car, but it's nicely updated to the new Chevy. Just rename the file NASC94.PCX, go to Paint Kit, select the first car, and then click on Import.

NFL CAR-SET   NFLCARS

This one's just for fun. Some of the designs are a bit crude, while others are nicely done. Judge for yourself. All 30 teams are represented with cars driven by a star player.

1995 WINSTON CUP CAR-SET   ACARS95

An excellent re-creation of the 1995 season from Dave Upson. The graphics are lovely, and the racing is tight and accurate.

This set has been updated throughout the 1995 season to reflect the point standings, driver changes, new teams, and new cars.

NASCAR GREATS SET   ALLTIME2
Ride with me now into the thrilling days of yesteryear, when NASCAR was still ruled by former moonshine runners and all-around bad boys. This outstanding set lets you race against the all-time greats of NASCAR, including Curtis Turner, Junior Johnson, Ned Jarrett, Fireball Roberts, and Fred Lorenzon. Lots of modern-era drivers are included, too, such as Richard Petty, David Pearson, Cale Yarborough, and Bobby Allison. The graphics are authentic and stunningly rendered. You *must* have this car-set. We all owe Manuel Daskalos a big thanks for this one.

BUSCH GRAND NATIONAL SET   95BGN#1
This racing series, just one small step below Winston Cup, regularly showcases some of the closest, most exciting racing in the country. A personal favorite of mine, this top-notch set faithfully re-creates the Busch cars and drivers. You'll want these car graphics, even if you don't want to race the Busch series.

INTERNATIONAL RACE OF CHAMPIONS   IROC95
You've seen it on television, now you can race in this prestigious series against champions from different racing series—guys like Earnhardt, Unser, and Pruett. This outstanding set from Dave Upson has it all: 12 Dodge Avengers, a "calendar" file to run the short IROC series, and a "drivers2.txt" file edited to make the racing as competitive as possible.

TOURING CAR CHAMPIONSHIP SET   DTM
This one's for you *NASCAR Racing* fans in Europe. The German International Touring Car Championship series is complete with accurate car models and driver names, according to author Georg Naujoks.

STARS AND STRIPES CAR   NEWOLDDO
This is one of the prettiest original designs you'll find. Bright, crisp, and colorful, this car just might become your new ride on the NASCAR circuit. Created by Kris Kaminski.

Figure 9.3
You'll find the legends of NASCAR in the All-Time car-set. Here's Ned Jarrett's #11 Chevy.

STREET CARS   **CARS**

There are plenty of street cars available for download, and this four-car set is a good place to start. You get an Eagle Talon, a Chevrolet Caprice painted as a police cruiser, and a Volvo sedan. If that's not enough, how about the Ford Taurus driven by Robocop?

MORE STREET CARS   **STREET**

More fun with car graphics. Here you'll find a Honda Civic, a Ford Taurus, a couple of Chevy Camaros, and a Ford Thunderbird. Very nicely done, and worth the download.

UTILITIES

In this section you'll find programs that allow you to change settings and edit just about every aspect of *NASCAR Racing*. These useful programs will help you set up your car, determine the relative strength of the computer cars, or just let you run all your races at night.

SET-UP SHEET   **SETUP**

A set-up sheet in the Windows Write format gives you quick access to your car set-ups for printing, comparison, and quick editing. By Rich Nagel.

Figure 9.4
The IROC series can give you a fun break from the rigors of a NASCAR season. Check out those Dodge Avengers.

TRACK RECORD UPDATE   **TRECORDS**
This program updates the lap record information shown that's displayed in the graphic when you choose a track. That graphic shows the best laps on that track, one for the player, and the other for computer cars. The computer records, though, aren't updated. This program fixes that omission. This version is for use with the Track Pack. By Rich Nagel.

SPEED AND TIME CALCULATOR   **SDT**
This program, from our friend Rich Nagel, calculates speed, distance, and time for all the tracks, including the Track Pack. A nice little program for racers who want to know more than just their lap speeds.

NIGHT RACING   **NCNIT121**
Rich Nagel has been at it again, editing *NASCAR Racing* to satisfy those nocturnal racers. This program changes the game's palette to look like you're running at night, or to put a covering of snow on the track. Very strange.

REPLAY EDITOR   **EDITRPY**
This excellent program gives you much more control over your library of race replays. You can cut and paste lap replays, and even superimpose them for comparison. There's also some

Figure 9.5
If you can't outrun Jeff Gordon, maybe you can just pull him over in this Chevrolet Caprice police cruiser.

solid lap analysis that produces data on time, distance, and acceleration.

NIGHT RACING   NIGHTIME
Here's an easy way to make any race a night race. It's a large program—471 K—but if you like running under the stars, check it out. By George Aker.

JEFF GORDON WALLPAPER   JGORDON
Here's some cool wallpaper for *NASCAR Racing* fans: Jeff Gordon's #24, rounding a corner on a road circuit. You also get a WAV file of a stock car accelerating out of a turn. By Chris Frederick.

CALENDAR   CALNDR95
This program updates the stock championship season to the 1995 schedule. It also fixes a bug in early versions of the Track Pack that caused some tracks to be omitted from the schedule. By Jeff Brown.

SET-UP UTILITY   NASSETUP
One of the most useful utilities available, this Windows program lets you quickly view, print, and compare different car set-ups. A must-have utility for you serious chassis experts.

SET-UP VIEWER   **VIEWSTG**

Another excellent set-up utility. With the click of your mouse you can view, print, export, and compare all STG set-up files.

WEIGHT VIEWER   **WEIGH-IT**

Weight distribution is the key to car set-up, and this program gives you some valuable insight into how your changes impact the weight borne by each wheel. Rear bias, left bias, and wedge are all used to calculate the weight on each tire. By Richard Cole.

DRIVER EDITOR   **ED10**

This is a fairly powerful editor that lets you change driver information, swap car positions, set driver style, and check the list for the proper PCX file. At 440 K, it's a big file, but it's well worth the download time. By Jim Smith.

DRIVER EDITOR   **DRVED2**

Another full-blown driver editor, this program allows you to sort drivers like you want them to run—fastest to slowest—and then automatically calculates new ratings. By C. J. Mahnken.

NEOPAINT PALETTE   **NASCAR**

If you want to try your hand at creating or editing car graphics in NeoPaint, you need this file. Paint Kit uses only 160 colors, instead of the 256 in a standard NeoPaint palette. Put the file in your NeoPaint directory and load it with the Edit Palette command. By D. Feeley.

PAINT KIT TEMPLATES   **NASTEM**

The easiest way to create your own cars in Paint Kit is to start with blank templates. This file gives you templates for the Pontiac Gran Prix, the Ford Thunderbird, and the Chevrolet Lumina and Monte Carlo. By Rich Nagel.

CAR SET-UPS

Set-ups are a very personal thing. What works for somebody else might be fast for you, or it might prove impossible to control. The surest way to develop a set-up that suits your driving

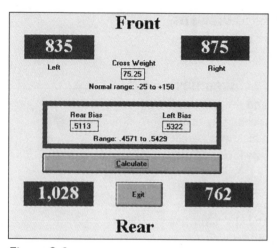

Figure 9.6
With the Weigh-it program, you can instantly see how weight is distributed in a set-up.

style is to start with the stock Ace set-up and work from there. But since we're all trying to get a little faster, we've included a sampling of set-ups on the disk.

YOU'RE NOT ALONE

You've been laboring all alone at your computer, trying to recreate David Pearson's Wood Brothers Mercury in the Paint Kit or trying to figure out how to get around the Phoenix raceway. You need help. Getting this book is a good start, and I hope I've helped you get more out of *NASCAR Racing*.

But you're not alone. There's a whole world of NASCAR racers out there in cyberspace. You'll find these guys hanging out in gaming and motorsports forums on all the on-line services and on the Internet. Whether you're on American Online, Prodigy, or CompuServe, there's plenty of valuable support that's yours for the taking.

FORUMS

This is where NASCAR gamers meet to swap stories, ideas, and tips. You'll learn a lot just by reading the "conversations" of the veteran drivers, set-up experts, and Paint Kit pros. But you'll get more out of it if you join the forum and begin asking questions. These cyberspace racers are a friendly bunch, and they'll be quick with advice and valuable information. You'll find racing forums on all the major on-line services.

LIBRARIES

After you get to know some of the on-line gamers, turn to the file libraries to find tons of graphics, utilities, and help files for *NASCAR Racing*. I've tried to give you the best files and programs available. But there's much more available, especially in the Motorsports library in the Sports Simulation forum on CompuServe.

RACING LEAGUES

Say you can't find a modem partner, to let you test your superior driving skills against a real human opponent? Don't despair. Once again, you can turn to the on-line racing community to help enhance your racing career.

There are a few on-line clubs that provide a way for players to compete against one another. Probably the most successful is NCAR, which "meets" in the Racing Circuits area of CompuServe's Sports Simulations forum. I'll give you an overview of how NCAR works. If you're interested in joining, post a message in the forum and you'll be racing against these guys right away.

NCAR OVERVIEW

This is an honor-based racing series, so if you can't play without cheating, then don't bother. Players race a schedule of events, running races under the same weather conditions and within the same parameters. The drivers then submit the results, which are then compared and scored to determine a winner and the overall finishing order. Keep in mind that the rules and procedures detailed below might have changed when you join.

Figure 9.7
Join an on-line racing club, and this battle against computer drivers will be translated into competition against real people.

THE RULES

Some settings are specific to the race, such as weather conditions, opponent strength, number of laps, and the size of the field. Other rules are the same wherever you're racing. You can't save and restart a race, though pausing is allowed. All races are run with Car Damage, Yellow Flags, and Pace Lap options turned on.

APPROVED CAR-SETS

You can use any car graphics you like, but the "drivers2.txt" file must have the same performance values as the original Cars94 file. There are several car-sets available on CompuServe that conform to this rule, and they're usually labeled "NCAR legal."

DON'T DIE YET!

GET THE OFFICIAL STRATEGY GUIDE FROM

S&S GAMES

By **OFFICIAL**, we mean reviewed, approved and endorsed by the same people who spent years in dark rooms creating this cool stuff.

With an **S&S GAMES GUIDE** you get the real scoop—an insider's take on how to become the grand master of the games you love. Oh yeah, you'll also stop dying all the time!

Sybex covers all the best-sellers. With complete maps, walk-throughs, strategies, secret cheat codes, and CD-ROMS packed with free game demos. **THESE BOOKS RULE.** So could you. Are you an S&S Games book collector yet? You will be.

Look for these Strategies & Secrets guides at your favorite software or bookstore today:

MECHWARRIOR 2 STRATEGIES & SECRETS
by Bernie Yee
0-7821-1857-7, Available NOW

APACHE STRATEGIES & SECRETS
by Andy Reese
0-7821-1865-8, Available NOW

STAR RANGERS STRATEGIES & SECRETS
by Dan Irish
0-7821-1870-4, Coming in February 1996

CAPITALISM STRATEGIES & SECRETS
by Larry Russell
0-7821-1871-2, Coming in February 1996

DUKE NUKEM 3D STRATEGIES & SECRETS
by Jonathan Mendoza
0-7821-1794-5, Coming in March 1996

INDYCAR RACING II STRATEGIES & SECRETS
by Steve Smith
0-7821-1897-6, Coming in March 1996

SYBEX